THE RAVINGS OF A RENEGADE

BEING THE WAR ESSAYS OF HOUSTON STEWART CHAMBERLAIN

Translated from the German by
CHARLES H. CLARKE, Ph.D.

With an Introduction by
LEWIS MELVILLE

LONDON
JARROLD AND SONS

INTRODUCTION.

It is with much pleasure that I write a few lines to introduce Dr. Clarke's translation of Mr. Houston Stewart Chamberlain's "Kriegsaufsätze" ("War Essays"). Dr. Clarke, who has spent many years in Germany, has a very wide knowledge of the language, the people, and the life of that country, and the reader may rest assured that the translation conveys the spirit of the original.

Mr. Houston Stewart Chamberlain, who was born in 1855, was intended for the British army—a circumstance which it is now amusing to remember—but being of delicate health and unable to endure the vagaries of the English climate, he went abroad, and has spent most of his days, first in Austria, and since 1900 in Germany. He married the daughter of Richard Wagner, and has written several books on German literature and music. In this country his best known work is "Die Grundlagen des neunzehnten Jahrhunderts," a translation of which appeared under the title of "The Foundations of the Nineteenth Century." When the war broke out, Mr. Chamberlain was invited by his friends to address himself to England and point out the wrong which that country had done in taking up arms against Germany; but, as he tells us, though he desired to do so, his pen absolutely declined to indite a word. He then bethought himself of telling Germany what he thought of England, and, lo! the sentences rolled over each other in their anxiety to be enrolled in that noble cause. These essays appeared in various periodicals; two of them, "England" and "Germany," were re-issued and circulated as a pamphlet; and all of them were collected and published in volume form. The book was accorded a very hearty welcome throughout Germany, and the copy in front of me bears the imprint, "seventh edition."

It may, of course, be held by some that no good purpose is served by presenting these essays in an English dress. I venture, however, to contend that the book is of great interest to British readers. I do not propose to discuss the taste of an Englishman who at such a time as this can abuse his country in the vitriolic style employed by Mr. Chamberlain: I merely assert that the "Kriegsaufsätze" are valuable as giving a clear insight into the Pan-German mind, in its most wild moments. Like all renegades, Mr. Chamberlain is *plus royaliste que le roi.* In his eyes everything in Germany is good, everything in England vile; virtue is German, culture is German, large-heartedness is German, literature and art are German, decadence and incompetence and vice and stupidity are English. In fact, he echoes the refrain of Herr Lissauer's infamous (but to British folk amusing) "Hymn of Hate": "We have only one enemy—England."

"As I believe in God, so do I believe in the holy German language," is the text of one of Mr. Chamberlain's essays. In another article he writes in all seriousness, "My conviction is that in all Germany during the last forty years there has not lived a single German who has wished for war—not one. Who puts forward the contrary view, lies—either deliberately or unintentionally." In a third paper he asks, "Why do all nations hate Germany and the Germans?" Mr. Chamberlain argues that this is due partly to envy, partly to misconception. The correct explanation is, however, to be found in another direction. Germany is hated because it can produce writers who are so fatuous as to put forward such opinions as are contained in this book, for it must be remembered that while the words are Mr. Chamberlain's, the sentiments he voices are those of almost the entire educated and "cultured" classes in the unhappy country which has adopted him.

LEWIS MELVILLE.

LONDON,
November 29th, 1915.

TRANSLATOR'S PREFACE.

In publishing a translation of Houston Stewart Chamberlain's "War Essays," it is perhaps necessary, from the very first, to make clear to the public that it is not an attempt to carry on German propaganda in our own country. It is certainly a most regrettable and painful fact that an Englishman should have been found capable of championing the worst form of Pan-German militarism, but it seemed impossible to allow a work emanating from such a quarter and containing so violent an attack on England to pass unheeded and unchallenged—especially in consideration of the vogue it has enjoyed in Germany, where, in spite of its exaggerated assertions and absolutely idiotic statements concerning English life and institutions, it is regarded as the last word of truth. It is read and commented on by everyone. A special edition of the two essays, "England" and "Germany," has been published as "Schützengrabenausgabe" (Trench Edition), and is supplied to the troops by thousands, the price of the copy being then reduced to the insignificant sum of thirteen pfennigs (about a penny three farthings). It is one of the principal items of a group of publications written by Sven Hedin, Ludwig Ganghofer, and Paul Oscar Höcker, which Germany with her accustomed thoroughness has mobilised against her enemies in the field. But, unlike his colleagues, Chamberlain has, as yet, not proceeded to the front. Like the General Staff in Berlin, for which he evinces such extravagant veneration, he sits in his study at Bayreuth, the holy seat of classic Wagnerism, and hurls one after another his bolts against Germany's enemies, destined, in his opinion, to have the same effect in the world of letters as the

Germans believe they have produced by their 43 cm. mortars in the war and to stagger humanity by the "frightfulness" of their irresistible logic. The purpose of this translation is to show the nature and quality of this logic, to reveal the tactics by which this renegade strategist proceeds to annihilate his native country and all her allies and to defend the country of his adoption. To do this it was necessary, though painful, to place the Essays in their entirety before the reading public.

In their essence the Essays are a defence, for every German—and I believe Chamberlain will feel honoured to be counted among them—finds himself in a state of hopeless defence as soon as he ventures to write on the German political attitude in the present war. But Chamberlain has studied strategy from the famous Field-Marshal Moltke and knows "der Hieb ist die beste Parade" ("the blow is the best defence"); he therefore allows no opportunity to escape, however remote it may be, without turning it into a stick with which to belabour his unfortunate native country. German and English literature are ransacked from their origins to the present day to rake up any comment, however trivial, derogatory to England or laudatory to Germany. It is interesting to note that all the witnesses called, both for the defence and the prosecution, are long since deceased; they are the most convenient category, unable to turn round and repudiate or qualify their testimony.

A country which produced Luther and Goethe must necessarily, according to Chamberlain, be destined to great things, and cannot possibly stray from the straight path of righteousness. Shakespeare, although admittedly a great genius, was, like Chamberlain, born in England. But then England has changed completely since that time. It has changed because it harbours two races—the Norman and the Anglo-Saxon—within its shores, which have never mingled, but throughout the centuries remained distinct in manners, speech, and attitude of mind. For Chamberlain the key of the whole present position lies in the Norman Conquest of the year 1066 and in a "turn of fate" which induced the honest Anglo-Saxon husbandman to leave his field and venture on "the dark and stormy deep," of which by nature he had an innate dread; for the sake of wealth to become a pirate, a trader.

Politically, England never flourished except in Anglo-Saxon times. Her Parliament has ruined her, as, in Chamberlain's opinion, all Parliaments ruin nations who are foolish enough to adopt them. Chamberlain would probably have recommended the retention of the "folkmote," which seems to be in his mind when he speaks of the future political institutions which are to be realised in Germany, when she has overthrown all her enemies and become the leading state in the world.

These constructive remarks of Chamberlain are not unlikely to cause him some trouble, when the heat of battle has passed away, for the reactionary spirit expressed in them is too evident and pronounced to be palatable even to the most docile German. But, in the meanwhile, any stick is good enough with which to beat a dog.

Burke, Bolingbroke, and Carlyle are all pressed into the ranks that are arrayed against us, especially Carlyle. But it is not the Carlyle of the "French Revolution," but the author of the "Life of Frederick the Great" and the "Essays on German Literature"—books which have long since been superseded in this country—with whom we have to contend. An essay on "Der Neue Kurs," the new course of German politics since the dismissal of Bismarck, by Carlyle, would certainly be of extreme interest, and Chamberlain might find himself in the same position as the sorcerer's apprentice in Goethe's "Zauberlehrling":

"Die ich rief, die Geister
Werd' ich nun nicht los."

("I cannot lay the spirits
Which I conjured up.")

The same would apply to Goethe. If the quotations derogatory to the German people by him and other well-known German poets and writers were to be collected, they would fill a handsome volume, without including those of Heinrich Heine, for whom Chamberlain, for obvious reasons, possesses little love; these might be bound up in a separate volume, there is no lack of them. Chamberlain is an arduous student of comparative philology and, as such, is doubtlessly acquainted with the works of a certain Max Müller, related to German poets of the same surname; perhaps in studying him he may have come across the lines:

"Auf Deutsch will ich es kühnlich sagen
Ohn' England wär die Weltnichtzu ertragen."

("I will boldly state in German that without
England the world would be unbearable.")

We see ourselves humbly forced to admit that Germany surpasses us in renegades, "comme en toute chose."

Seriously, Chamberlain is a man of extensive learning and great literary attainments, which he has displayed in his works on "The Foundations of the Nineteenth Century," on "Kant," on "Goethe," all of which are written in the "holy German language," the only tongue, we presume, capable, by means of its structure and "contents," of conveying the thoughts of the author in an adequate form. He lives at Bayreuth, which, by the way, is the only place, even in Germany, in which he could possibly live. He is connected by marriage with the family of the great composer, Richard Wagner.

It is absolutely necessary to bear these facts in mind in order to understand the Essays and judge them in their right *milieu.*

No man of any artistic feeling can withstand the charm of transcendental music, which appeals to that part of the human soul which, in ordinary life, leads a half-famished existence, and in many cases has ceased to exist for want of nutriment. But it is like the flame of which Schiller speaks in his "Song of the Bell": "Wehe, wenn sie losgelassen!" ("Woe, when untrammelled it escapes our guard.") From the oppressed it turns into the tyrant. The mind then turns entirely to the pursuit of the universal, which, because it is itself of a dual constitution—like the English nation—it is unable to assimilate. It becomes unable to appreciate the facts of everyday life, to understand itself or those surrounding it, and loses itself in the dim vagueness of sentimentality—*Irrlichterei-Schwefelei*, as the Germans express it.

It was particularly against this attitude of mind that Goethe, after having overcome it in his youth, in the period of storm and stress, contended during the rest of his long life, fixing as his ideal the harmony between the individual and the universal, in the soul of man—this being its most natural, most human and, therefore, highest state.

The poet may be granted an excess of the "universal"; for him who writes on scientific, economic, or political questions it is far safer to err on the other side.

This has repeatedly been brought home to Chamberlain by his German critics, so that he has been forced to turn and face them in a defence. At present he probably believes he can let himself go with impunity; zeal for the good cause will excuse all lack of scientific exactitudes.

But still we fear his Essay, "The German Language," will cause as much head-shaking in the ranks of scientific Germanic philology as his wild political assertions among cool-headed politicians and diplomatists, to say nothing of his praise of Luther in the ranks of the powerful Central Party (Roman Catholic) in Germany and the clerical party in Austria. Things must indeed have changed if these gentlemen are to stand quietly by and be told that they, although remaining true to their old faith, have profited immensely in religion, morals, and national life by the work of Martin Luther.

A later Essay called "Die Zuversicht" ("Confidence")—not included in this collection—shows that he has had to defend himself against the accusation of flattering the German people. But these are things between him and his adopted Fatherland.

Much more serious is the manner in which he treats the political events which led up to the war. Nowhere does he make the slightest attempt to prove the base charges he brings against his native country. It is sufficient for him to say, "as is well known," "as is accepted." In this respect, as in all others, he forms the exact antithesis to his countryman by adoption, the author of "J'accuse," and I should strongly recommend a minute comparison of the two books. In fact, it is difficult for an Englishman to understand why the author of "J'accuse" should go to such trouble to prove things that are self-evident, until he is confronted with amazing accusations brought forward by a representative of German opinion in the style of Chamberlain. All Chamberlain's accusations against England on account of her self-seeking policy are conclusively refuted in the chapters of "J'accuse" dealing with this subject, and the statistical material is supplied.

But Chamberlain goes still farther. He hints that England was a party to the foul murder of the heir to the Austrian throne; that the whole of the British fleet was mobilised in July, 1914, in anticipation of events which those in power were trying to bring about. He states that a friendly visit by the British fleet to Kiel was undertaken for the express purpose of spying, as all other means to attain knowledge of this harbour had failed. A man born of British parents and on British soil who can do that places himself outside the pale. He exposes himself to be regarded as the paid agent of a hostile state, and many will maintain that the "iron cross" which decks his bosom is not the only reward he has received for fouling his own nest; but that "klingende Münze" ("hard cash"), to use the pretty German expression, has also played its part. And what, after all, can be said against this assertion? Has not Chamberlain proved, to his own full satisfaction, that an Englishman will do anything for money? True, Warren Hastings did not seek to enrich himself, but his company, his country. Chamberlain admits this. But then, that was a long time ago, and we are on the downward grade and must have travelled considerably since then.

It is dangerous to cut away the ground beneath one's own feet; the slightest move, and one falls into the precipice—the bottomless pit. Rightly did Schiller say:

"Ans Vaterland, ans teure schliess dich an
Da sind die starken Wurzeln deiner Kraft."

("Adhere unto thy native land,
For from there thy strength doth come.")

Curious, this applies to an Englishman just as much as to a German!

Even the greatest of tacticians occasionally make mistakes. A slight detail is overlooked, a loophole is left by which the enemy may break through and reach the very heart of the position. This accident would appear to have happened to our strategic author in spite of his attack, distinguished by so much brilliant impetuosity—"durch seinen flotten Schneid," as he would express it, or, perhaps, exactly on this account.

When extolling the intrinsic merits of the General Staff he states that the whole plan of the campaign of 1914 was drawn up by the Great Field-Marshal Helmuth von Moltke, who died in the year 1891. This plan was modernised and kept in readiness by the General Staff. But it must necessarily have contained the passage of the German troops through Belgium and the breach of Belgian neutrality. But this, according to Chamberlain, was justified by a convention between France and Belgium, formed in the reign of Edward VII., who ascended the throne in 1902. There is a German proverb, "Allzu scharf macht schartig" ("Too sharp turns the edge"), and Chamberlain would do well to be more careful how he deals with the secrets entrusted to him by his friends of the General Staff.

But now for the lighter vein, which, fortunately, is never entirely missing, especially when learned gentlemen of Chamberlain's calibre descend into the sphere of ordinary life.

It is long since I have enjoyed anything so much as Chamberlain's description of a London Christmas festival. The families, seated at thousands of tables in the dining halls of the London hotels, awaiting the stroke of twelve to sing "For he's a jolly good fellow," and indulge promiscuously in dancing the "Tango," is a picture that deserves to live; and it will live in Germany, handed down from father to son. I don't quite understand why they should wait till midnight; there would appear to be some slight confusion between Christmas and New Year—they follow each other with such overwhelming rapidity. But, nevertheless, it is a pearl.

Not less amusing is Chamberlain's hunt for a blue tie throughout the whole of London when blue was out of fashion. Hard lines! To say nothing of the English town of forty thousand inhabitants in which not a single person was to be found who could read words of four syllables without floundering, or of Chamberlain's journey through the deserted streets of the capital on boat-race day. They are all classical and will be told and told again to our children when travelling on the Continent.

We offer our deepest sympathy to Mr. Chamberlain at the shock he received on hearing of the British Association, referred to as the "British Ass," and would recommend him not to expose his nerves to such a trial again without the utmost necessity. In short, we rather fear that his humour has not survived his long sojourn in Bayreuth. Our humour has stuck to us in spite of our general depravity. Perhaps it is the last remnant of Merry Old England, and while there is humour there is still life. It proves, at least, that our minds are still healthy and capable of that harmony which Goethe considered so essential. For it is humour which, as the electric spark springing from cloud to cloud equalises the two poles, mediates in the soul of man between the individual and the universal and produces the pure air of harmony—a fresher and a purer atmosphere than would appear to prevail at Bayreuth at present.

CONTENTS.

I.

GERMANY'S LOVE OF PEACE.

I.

GERMANY'S LOVE OF PEACE.

In these holy days of such grave import there is no inclination for the niceties of style; even the oratory of Demosthenes sounds hollow in comparison with the deed of laying down one's life for the Fatherland. Facts alone are of interest to us at the present moment. "Facts," says Carlyle, "go beyond thought; beside them words are but stammering and stuttering." But how are we to arrive at facts? Material ones, true, force themselves upon us, but how do we contrive to obtain intellectual, moral facts? The monstrous fact of the European War is borne in upon us by day and night; but what fact lies at the root of this war? Who desired it? The enemies of Germany maintain that Germany is the breaker of the peace, there will be no lasting peace till Germany be destroyed; whence this conception of a demented brain? How is it possible to hide from the sight of millions the evident truth, the "fact"? He who says fact presupposes truth. An untrue fact is void; an "ens imaginarum"; Kant's "empty apperception without an object"; but at times this void imagination contrives to gain a demoniacal power over the ideas of man.

By means of the Press, which can do so much to spread the truth, mendacity has, in the hands of few individuals, grown to a power beyond conception throughout the world; we see it drastically in the war news published in the foreign press, and yet how harmless are lying reports of victories in comparison with the systematic poisoning of a whole nation by a plan of lying which has been carefully thought out and carried on for years.

Oscar Wilde once wrote an essay on the "Art of Lying." Since then his countrymen have made considerable progress in this noble art. This does not imply that the statesmen of former times followed the straight path of open honesty; but cunning was met by cunning, the fox was out-foxed, and, thus, it can, in a certain sense, be said that the trickery of a Richelieu, for instance, was "honest cheating." But now the entirely unsuspecting are misled.

No statesman of the present day can ignore public opinion; it is impossible—at least to the West of the Dwina—to carry on a war, if the great masses of the people are not persuaded of its necessity; and, as no civilised people of their own free will desire war, the necessity—a matter which Richelieu could dispense with—must be demonstrated to them.

Here a terrible thing is revealed; lies have exactly the same effect as truth, for they are believed. It is sufficient to acquire a certain number of papers with large circulation and consequently of great influence, to place them under a united management and, in a few years, the purpose is attained. Never in the history of the world has the deception of an entire nation been so shamefully, so wickedly, conceived and carried out as the deception of England in regard to Germany. This deception alone is responsible for the present war. From the very beginning England, the dynamic force, desired the war and brought it about; England caused the estrangement between Russia and Germany; England has incessantly egged on France to war. This criminal policy was possible, solely by means of a well-calculated, systematic deception of the English people.

The chief agitator was a king, the mental tool of a soulless, cunning diplomatist, who worshipped the ancient English principle that in matters of state hypocrisy and mendacity are the most effective arms; as "manager" of the plot a clever journalist was selected to whom all opinions were indifferent as long as they brought him profit. At this period he already possessed papers of the most various political opinions, he acquired more and more; ultimately the *Times*, whose course he had long controlled, passed into his hands; to-day, parading with the title of a Lord which hides his real name and his un-English descent, he rules supreme throughout the English Press. To mention one thing: for years the reports of the *Times* correspondent in Berlin have been a disgrace; this man without a conscience—on whose cowardly head a great quantity of all the misery of the war falls—has by positive and negative lying surpassed the limit of imagination. Repeatedly I asked why the villain was not hounded from Berlin to the frontier; the reply was: There is no law against lying. Such a law must be made! Liars who endanger the peace of Europe must be hanged.

And now, after dealing with the fictitious fact that Germany desired the war, we turn to the real fact: Germany was the guardian of the peace. My testimony as a foreigner may bear some weight in this respect.

For forty-five years my intercourse has been mainly with Germans; for thirty years I have lived constantly in Germany; the love of German character, German thought, German science, German art, has sharpened my sight without making me blind to her faults. My judgment has remained entirely objective; and to many things which displeased me the day I set foot on German soil I have never been able to accustom myself. From earliest youth in close relations to France, attached to England by bonds of blood, I regarded all countries with an unbiassed eye. It is true I have led a secluded life, have never sought by vulgar sight-seeing and running after celebrities to acquire a knowledge of the country and people, but things are seen more distinctly at a distance than at close range; in silence the ear hears more clearly than in the midst of confusing din. And my testimony is: *in the whole of Germany during the last forty-three years not a single man has lived who desired war; no, not a single one.* He who maintains the contrary lies—be it consciously or unconsciously.

I have had the good fortune to become acquainted with Germans from all parts of the Empire and of all spheres of life, from Imperial Majesty to the honest artisan, with whom I have had daily dealings. I have known intimately schoolmasters, scholars, merchants, bankers, officers, diplomatists, engineers, poets, journalists, officials, artists, physicians, lawyers. Never have I met a warlike one or, to be more exact, one eager for war. But in England, during my last visits in 1907 and 1908, everywhere an absolutely horrifying hatred of Germany and the impatient expectation of a war of destruction. The absence of animosity to other nations is the most striking characteristic of the Germans—and of the Germans alone. They generally err on the side of exaggerated recognition of foreign merits. Besides, every German knows that, owing to the geographical position of his country, he has everything to fear and nothing to hope for from a war. How should a people whose industry, trade, and science were thriving more and more every year, as was the case with Germany during the last forty-three years, wish to bring on a war which must destroy all three?

I will now only say a few words more about the Emperor William.

He alone, as an individual, could give the definite decision. I have not met the Emperor frequently, but under particularly favourable circumstances, beyond the bonds of court etiquette, unobserved, in informal interchange of opinion; I have never repeated a word of the monarch; not that he entrusted any secrets to me, but because one can never foresee the possible effect of a word spoken by a man in so exposed a position; nor will I to-day renounce my maxim. Yet I commit no indiscretion when I say that in this important personality two traits appeared to me specially remarkable, as the two "dominants" of all his feeling, thinking, acting: the deep and never relaxing feeling of responsibility before God and—closely and exactly defined by this—the energetic, masterful, yes—should it not sound too paradoxical—the turbulent desire to preserve peace for Germany.

Germany's power, which he has done so much to foster, was not to conjure up a war, but enforce peace on all ill-wishers. His actions, indeed, bear evidence of it; for, when, during the last ten years the situation became nearly unbearable for Germany's honour—and England took good care that this should be the case—it was he who again and again prevailed for peace. Not that there was ever a war party in Berlin—

that is a lie of the *Times*; but there were responsible ministers and soldiers who said: If England and her companions wish for war at any price, then let it be at once. But the Emperor could not let this argument prevail with his conscience. He thrust the half-drawn sword into its sheath.

No wish—of that I am entirely persuaded—stood higher with him than the wish to be able to say on his death-bed: I have inviolably preserved the peace of my country, history will call me the "Emperor of Peace." If God gives the Austro-German arms the complete, overwhelming victory for which we all pray, even we who are not Germans, in so far as we value the attainments of civilised humanity higher than national vanity, then, and only then, will Europe enjoy a century of peace, and the wish of the great and good monarch, who has been so shamefully deceived by his fellow-princes, will yet be fulfilled more gloriously than he himself had thought; at the same time a justification for all Germany against slander and lying. Then, more intensely, will he be called the "Emperor of Peace," as he and his army have created peace as their own brave achievement.

II.

GERMAN LIBERTY.

II.

GERMAN LIBERTY.

The assertion that Germany's enemies are fighting for liberty against tyranny is to be found with striking frequency in official manifestos and newspaper articles. The opinion has long been circulated throughout the world that everywhere where Germany goes there is an end to all freedom. I have met serious men, scholars in England, for instance, who had warm sympathy for German science and literature, and yet believed that, politically, it would be a misfortune if Germany's influence were to increase in Europe, for it would mean the destruction of all liberty.

Now when I occasionally attempted, in

oral disputes to support the contrary, that Germany had, for centuries, been the real and sole home of a liberty which tends to raise the human race and is alone worthy of the name, I never succeeded in rousing interest. The English and French, even the well-educated, do not reflect on the essence of liberty, on its peculiar function in the complicated organism of the human mind; for them it is purely a political idea which has been handed down through the ages; they always considered they had refuted me when they brought out as trumps that the German Imperial Chancellor was appointed and retained by the Emperor, and could remain in office in spite of the majority of the Reichstag. The essence of liberty is, therefore, to be able to overthrow chancellors. Whole books would be necessary to give real enlightenment on this subject—to destroy wrong ideas and replace them by correct ones. I will only make a few remarks, give a little food for reflection.

Let us ask first: In what does the far-famed English political liberty really consist? If one were to sum up the internal history of England, which, till 1688, was heroic and sanguinary, and later on Machiavellian and intriguing, in a single formula, it would be: History of a struggle between nobility and crown. Neither of these factors thought of liberty; each only sought to increase its power. When Cromwell appeared, both joined issue against the one man, and the sole course which would have been capable of founding true freedom in England. Afterwards the course, thanks to the insular position of the country, was very simple, and from it rose the English Parliament, which has been set up as an unattainable pattern till one is tired of hearing of it, and in which, until a few years ago, the Lower House was just as aristocratic as the Upper House. For a long time England has been ruled by an oligarchy, the king is a puppet. Up to the commencement of the nineteenth century the sovereign, if he possessed the necessary energy, had a say in the election of the Prime Minister, then he lost this prerogative, and the secret committee of the parliamentary oligarchy has since governed alone. The fiction of the two chief parties is still kept up, and the minority of the male population which enjoy the franchise still decide when the one shall be superseded by the other; but the leaders of both parties work under the same cover and keep at a distance all who might be inclined to restrict their power or the profits they derive. Offices are given only by the governing caste: the leader of the victorious party must be Prime Minister, and all other ministers are elected not, as one might presume, by the party, but by the secret committee; king and people have no say whatever in the matter. Discipline is severely maintained in the parties by the Whips; woe to any member who should dare to express his own opinion. The House of

Commons has, it is true, assumed a slightly more democratic appearance in consequence of the extension of the franchise, which was first carried out by Disraeli and then by Gladstone; but the system has remained unaltered; aristocracy is yielding to plutocracy. What the House has lost in gentility it has gained in power. The restriction of the freedom of speech, particularly by the introduction of the so-called "guillotine," which permits every debate to be broken off at a certain time and a vote to be taken at once, has transformed this pretended freest of all parliaments into a kind of machine, by means of which a small group of politicians rule and govern for seven years according to their own sweet will. The tyranny of this clique, which, as the recent Marconi scandal proved, are not even afraid of indulging in shady financial transactions, was rendered complete when, two years ago, a decisive influence on the legislation was withdrawn from the Upper House. The veto-right of the crown has long ago fallen into abeyance. And thus England is governed by a "Convent," or rather a "Conventicle." And that is called freedom!

But I should like to go deeper. For liberty is of a frail and tender nature, and often flees from public life to take up her abode in the energetic life of individuals; this may be observed in the United States. To a certain extent it is also the case in England. I do not believe there are so many cranks—people who take no heed of public opinion or custom, who care neither for good or bad reputation, but think, act, and live as it suits them personally—anywhere as in England. But these exceptions do but prove the rule, and in their grotesque particularities show the reverse of the general lack of liberty. The last time I was a few weeks in England I made my friends very angry because I could not help exclaiming, "You are truly a nation of sheep." It begins with the smallest habits of daily life, and continues up to political opinions, everything on the same pattern. Every man wears the same trousers; every woman the same bonnet; I remember that once in the whole of London not a single blue tie was to be had: blue was out of fashion; such a thing is impossible in Berlin, Paris, Vienna. All people of both sex read the same novels, devour one volume a day "the novels of the week." On the day of the boat race between Oxford and Cambridge one walks through literally empty streets in London; the oldest duchess and the youngest chimney-sweep, all are seized by the same enthusiasm, as by a madness, for this event, of which, at the best, they see but little, and, in no case, understand anything, as in order to understand the achievement a special knowledge of all kinds of details—tide, wind, etc.—is requisite, which is only possessed by expert oarsmen.

Closely allied to this sporting mania is a

complete contempt for all mental attainments. I am not only speaking of ignorance alone; truly, with the exception of the small class of exquisitely trained scholars, the ignorance is so immense that no German can form an idea of it; in a town of forty thousand inhabitants it was found impossible, five years ago, to find a single man capable of reading English correctly to a convalescent. They stumbled over words of three syllables and broke down entirely when they came to those of four! But of that I will not speak for the moment, but of the conscientious objection to every intellectual occupation which is prevalent in England. Years ago, the Swede, Steffens, remarked rightly (in his excellent book, "England as a World Power"): "The English seemed to have a superstitious dread of intellectual influences in the management of human affairs." Every well-educated man in England is suspicious; he only gains consideration the moment when his intellectual attainments begin to bring in money—otherwise, he is regarded as a fool.

A few years ago I arrived—unfortunately a few weeks too late—in a town where the annual meeting of the British Association had taken place; I was congratulating one of the principal inhabitants—an unusually talented man, decorated with many orders, esteemed at court, and known and admired in all quarters—on this meeting of the most important English scholars, and of many from abroad, which must have brought him stimulus and experience.

At first the gentleman in question did not understand me, then he said, laughing: "Oh, you mean the British Ass, as we call the Association. I am thankful to say I managed to keep so well out of the way of the gentlemen that I did not see one of them." It is thus that pure science is treated in England, in the best circles. I could give many such examples, interesting, because they are taken from life; but my main purpose is to point out that true liberty is incompatible with such a frame of mind: not only is English industry and manufacture, the whole spirit of public life, blighted by this hatred of culture, but it also destroys the possibility of liberty. Liberty, we know, since Kant is an idea, no man is born free; liberty must be acquired by each individual. Its accessories are an education and strengthening of the mind, a methodical uplifting above all with which it was originally endued, until that liberation is attained which alone deserves the name of liberty. External liberty, if not preceded by internal liberty, is but licence. The English understand by liberty the right to walk on the grass without being stopped by a policeman; that they are not restricted by military duties from setting out into the world in search of adventures; that they may leave school at an early age to act as clerk in a solicitor's office, and thus, without the troublesome compulsion of studying law, in a few years become a solicitor, etc., etc. On the other hand, the German may not walk on the grass; he may not arrange his life as it pleases him best; but he is obliged to sacrifice valuable years of youth and, later on, many holiday weeks to his Fatherland, and his life when the necessity arises. None of the higher professions are open to him unless he has acquired extensive general and specific knowledge. Is he, on this account less free than the Englishman? Does not the irresistible superiority of the German soldier lie in his moral qualities particularly? And what does this mean but that he acts of his own free will. He alone wishes what he is ordered to do, wishes it with his whole heart; the English, the French, the Russian soldier is ordered to do a thing which has no relation to his personal will; in the best of cases he only obeys a desire of destruction which, not natural to him, has been roused by a system of lies. And is it not their education which raises the German middle class above that of all other nations ? —the education which is enforced upon them by the nation with relentless severity, and thanks to which the individual becomes a person capable of free judgment. Even the numerous trifling annoyances, what may be done and what may not be done, which, at first, are very irksome to us foreigners in Germany, are they not at bottom the result of general good order from which all profit ? They may be exaggerated, but are, on the whole, a good school of discipline and consideration of others. Martin Luther teaches: "The flesh should have no liberty"; on the contrary, every man should be "servant of all." And then he continues: "But in the spirit and in our conscience we are most free from all servitude; there we believe no man, there we trust no man, put confidence in no man, fear no man but solely Jesus Christ." I do not know if the present-day Englishmen consider Martin Luther a free man; the great majority, even among the educated, know, I am afraid, as little about him as their king does about Goethe, probably no more than the name. And were I now to let Frederick the Great speak: "Without liberty there is no happiness," they would certainly object that he was a tyrant. We, on the other hand, experience how liberty is obtained. Liberty is no abstract quality, that hovers in the air, and for which one needs only to stretch out one's hand; that is mock liberty that is thus caught, a deceptive illusion that falling from the horn of Pandora vanishes into thin air.

German Freedom—real Freedom—was conceived and created by Martin Luther, Frederick, Kant, Goethe, Wilhelm von Humboldt, Bismarck, and thousands of others, who each, according to his strength, trod in the steps of these great creators of Freedom. An un-German liberty is no liberty. This Goethe knew right well when, towards 1792, he observed that "A certain desire for liberty, a striving for democracy," was beginning to gain possession of many German minds. "They did not seem to feel," he writes, "what they must lose first to attain some kind of questionable advantage." And bitterly he upbraids "this fluctuation of opinion—unfortunately the result of German character always prone to imitation."

Germany has attained this precious possession in the course of struggles—physical and mental—throughout centuries. This German freedom is an absolutely original product. Humanity has, up to the present, known nothing which resembles it. It stands incomparably higher than Hellenic liberty; besides, it is much more firmly founded than that ephemeric product which could resist neither the external enemy nor internal decay. Characteristic of German liberty is the conscious assertion of the whole. All individual parts of the empire preserve their independence and submit to be subjected to the whole. Thus, too, every man submits from infancy for the good of the whole. That is the first step to liberty.

This freedom, and only this, can hope for duration. For the first time in the history of the world, freedom, as an inclusive and continuous property, becomes possible. Let this, above all, be borne in mind. "Freedom is not licence but truthfulness," says Richard Wagner. But how can a whole commonweal, a whole nation in its political structure and character be no longer arbitrary but truthful? The sublime spectacle which Germany in the war of 1914 offers teaches us. Let that be compared with the trivial nonsense we hear from kings, ministers, orators, and poets. It is unnecessary to speak of the liberty Russia has to dispense; what liberty poor betrayed and ruined France can promise, the country of political corruption, of hollow words, needs as little explanation. England understands by liberty only the right of the mighty, and this right only for herself. Not a single spark of intellectual life has ever sprung from its immense colonial empire. The inhabitants are all only cattle-owners, slave-owners, merchandise accumulators, mine exploiters, and everywhere there reigns the absolute licence of brutality which develops everywhere where it is not opposed by intellectual culture : that brutality which Rudyard Kipling, England's most popular poet, has the front to claim as the highest power and greatest glory of England.

The continuance and development of freedom on earth depends on the victory of the German arms and on Germany's remaining true to herself after victory. And just as freedom in Germany though at first only the dream and hope of a few God-favoured men, and which even to-day can only be completely and consciously conceived by those who are favoured by nature and circumstances—nevertheless gradually permeates the whole people, as we now experience it in this war, when millions immediately rush to arms, who could not have been called upon, therefore by their own free will. In this same manner German freedom will spread over all the world as far as the German language sounds. True freedom will form a better glue than jingoism. And the German language—the holy warden of these mysteries—no longer despised and soon forgotten by her own children in far-off lands, but everywhere fostered and developed, will found a universal Teutonism, and by degrees educate other nations, in so far as nature has granted them the capacity, to understand liberty and thus enter into its possession.

God grant this victory.

III.

THE GERMAN LANGUAGE (LETTER TO E. E.).

III.

THE GERMAN LANGUAGE

(Letter to E. E.).

You are certainly right. It would be criminal, if just in these September days, when the great decision is pending which will decide all future issues, to abandon oneself to the intoxication of foolhardy confidence. From a thinking being, at least, more logic is to be expected than humbly to petition God for help and, at the same time, to be persuaded the Germans could not possibly fail to be victorious. I believe that the Germans have done everything humanly possible to emerge as victors from this struggle which has been forced upon them; but I know what part is played in history by insignificant circumstances, accidents, as they are called. From the bottom of my heart, I turn to God and say as our Saviour has taught us: "Father, not as I will; Thy will alone be done." True humility means to be prepared for all. Do we, indeed, know which would be more difficult to bear—victory or defeat?

And yet, how shall I express myself? I am afraid I shall become illogical or even impious. I could only regard a German defeat as a deferred victory. I should say to myself, the time is not yet ripe, we must continue to preserve the holy treasure in the restricted circle of the Fatherland. For Germany alone, at the present day, among all nations preserves a living, holy treasure, capable of development. It is inexpressible like all that comes from God, and I feel myself not only incapable of describing it or even of circumscribing it. One must be born a German, or have become one, to understand this; one must live in the midst of this manifold blessing, must breathe its air, work in its light, live in its sunshine, rest under its benevolent protection. And there the word of our so exclusively German Schiller occurs to me: "When once light has penetrated a man, there is no night outside." For the moment let these words suffice. What we call "German" is the secret by which mankind is enlightened; and the means of this enlightenment is the German language.

Nothing can persuade me that this language is destined to destruction! There are other languages rich in works of the spirit; who would deny it? I, least of all, who from infancy up to the present day have felt myself at home in English and in French, so that Shakespeare, Hume, and Sterne, Ronsard, Pascal, and Rousseau, are in their own words, their untranslatable idioms, nearly as accessible and familiar to my ear and understanding as Luther, Herder, and Goethe. I also possess a slight idea of the structure and vigour of the ancient languages; can read Italian, and owe lasting impressions to the study of Spanish and Serbo-Croatian. Based on this knowledge and other knowledge acquired from comparative philology, I maintain that, among living languages, German occupies, unquestionably, a unique position of majesty and vitality which excludes any comparison. This lies partially in the structure of the language, as it has been formed by history, partially in the products which it has received from an unparalleled series of virile, eminent, and partially heroic minds. These products—let this be added at once—transcend the realm of language. Thus, for instance, Johann Sebastian Bach, the marvel, whom Goethe can only compare with God, is unthinkable beyond the pale of the German language and beyond the lines which Luther indicated for the development of the spirit of this language. All this is but one and the same current.

In regard to its structure, so many excellent things have been said and so many things are treasured in your faithful memory that I can merely restrict myself to referring you to the fourth of Fichte's "Orations to the German Nation." On the whole, I must confess, I find Fichte difficult. He generally goes against my grain; but this lecture on "The principal differences between the Germans and other nations of Teutonic origin" I always read again from time to time, and derive benefit from it. First, I am pleased to see that he reckons among the "nations of Germanic origin the French, the Spaniards, and the Italians." It is quite evident how much Germanic blood must flow in their veins as the source of their vigour. It is sufficient to know what the idea "German" means, and to have studied a little history; and yet this evident truth stated in the winter-term, 1807-8, had to be rediscovered in our days. Secondly, Fichte pronounces in simple words an absolutely decisive fact by seeking the reason for the increasing differences between nations, above all, in their languages. Among the languages of Europe, German is the only living one. Everything else is deducted from this fact, for, as Fichte observes: "Between the living and the dead no comparison is possible, and the former has an infinite advantage over the latter," therefore all direct comparisons between the German language and the Neo-Latin languages are entirely void of sense and forced to treat of matters which are not worth the trouble. The catastrophe which has deprived all these languages of life—English forms no exception—is that they are founded on dead roots, that is to say, composed of dead material; therefore they were from the beginning artificial, not natural languages. These nations, Fichte rightly says, "have, exactly speaking, no native language," a fact for which Richard Wagner found the adequate expression: "Their language speaks for them, but they do not speak in their language." That is to say, the moment all words which do not designate only concrete things, but serve to express and communicate thought, are no longer derived from impressions known to the senses—when, for instance, "Erfolg" is expressed by "succès," and thus, in the place of a vivid idea of striving for a goal, crowned by the prefix "er" to indicate attainment, two syllables "suc" and "cès" stand, both of which for the present-day Frenchman have no signification. As soon as this takes place, words become only counters, incapable of inflexion, modulation, or composition; the ordinary man ceases to think and genius finds no instrument by which he can produce new thought, *la médiocrité est de rigeur*,—mediocrity is absolutely imposed. Whereas in a language which has retained its living qualities, like the German, "the transcendental part is metaphorical, comprising at every step the entire physical and mental life of the nation in complete unity, in order to express an idea which is not arbitrary but has resulted from the past life of the nation."

The fact must not be overlooked that the Latin language when, towards the end of the Republic, it became a language of culture, was forced to borrow; for it cannot be maintained as of the Greek that it is living; for it borrows from the Greek numerous terms for thoughts, sentiments, and ideas, ready made, as they had been coined during the centuries of the absolutely original development of the Hellenic races, and in the attempt to adapt native words to the foreign meaning, misunderstandings arose, from which we still suffer to-day. I need only refer you to the chapter on the word "Nature" in my book on Goethe. There were partial and complete misunderstandings; the Latin language of the classical period possessed consequently—the moment it rose above the sphere of everyday life—no living connection with the language of the people; it was an artificial language which was incomprehensible to the people, "half dead in its own home." The result of this is that the present languages of Western Europe spring from a doubly dead root. Besides the German, the Scandinavian languages alone have remained pure.

So much about the structure of the German language, just to refresh your memory. The German language is a living tongue, and because it lives it is fit to serve as a vessel for divine thought.

But now I beg you to direct your glance to the critical point at which the contents are poured into the vessel. "To the possessor of such a language the spirit speaks directly, and reveals itself to him, as one man to another," says Fichte; and Goethe exclaims: "Come, Holy Ghost, Thou all-creator, and visit all our souls!"

But to attain this many things are necessary. An individual spirit, here and there, capable of receiving and transmitting the revelations of the Holy Ghost is not sufficient. If the language is to derive strength, each of these favoured souls must belong to a national life on broad foundation, rich in forces, talents, and a passionate desire for activity; souls must be linked one to the other and one after another; language and thought are interdependent; they grow one upon the other; united they rise like a tree with spreading boughs. The Scandinavian languages form a valuable reserve, a kind of reinforcement behind the German lines; but their geographical position has refused an extensive and luxuriant expansion to these nations. But in Germany this expansion took place in an ideal manner. Let the historian deplore Germany's lack of unity, and the innumerable sufferings it has caused in times gone by. The intellectual life profited by it to attain the incomparable diversity of conditions and, therefore, the variety of determinating influences within the unity of experience and thought provided by the language. By this means the language was kept alive and remains so to-day. If you trace French from Rabelais and Montaigne down to Voltaire, you perceive an increasing impoverishment in the vocabulary as well as in the inflexions, until the structure has definitely been beaten to shining steel and functions mechanically. This development, which, regarded from a higher standpoint, is retrogressive, corresponds to the instinct of genius; as the language was artificial, there was only one means of attaining relative perfection—it must be entirely artificial—no trace of nature. A Montaigne at the present date must hold his peace—or learn German. I should like to call your special attention to the following: If this peculiar process led to an unprecedented result it was not due solely to the logical necessity of the linguistic position, but, to a great extent, to political development. The French language developed exactly on the lines of unity and sameness desired by the monarchy; the French Revolution might destroy the external Bastille, but not the internal; the spirit of this nation is for ever imprisoned. The German language, too, has suffered many losses in vocabulary and idioms since the days of Martin Luther; particularly the unfortunate prevalence of Latin among the educated classes till about 1750 had a destructive effect. It was exactly this political diversity which, together with the essential properties of the language, averted a catastrophe.

One need but cast a glance on Upper and Lower Austria, on Styria, on Switzerland, on the Low German provinces, to perceive what treasures of living words and idioms were preserved. Thanks to the political disunity, these remained capable, at any moment, of once more becoming common property of the nation. A large proportion of the present-day vocabulary has been preserved from threatening oblivion in the course of the eighteenth century by the works of Gottsched, Adelung, and their contemporaries and successors. Leibnitz, in his "Unvorgreifliche Gedanken" ("Essays without Prejudice") indicated the way; Goethe and Richard Wagner boldly returned to the original roots, but much remained to be done in this respect. It is an inestimable blessing that political notion and language did not coincide. He is a German who speaks the German tongue. No nation of the present or the past—except the Greeks—can compare in rich diversity with German. And upon this fertile soil the spirit has revealed itself continuously for centuries so that the thought expressed in German now occupies a unique position in the world.

It is of supreme importance that the beginnings of the German language reach, without interruption, back into antiquity. This is the foundation of the living roots of which I spoke above. A similar state exists in no other language of the present time, at least in no language of literature—French, particularly, shows in its very origin an arbitrary development dependent on chance. It developed as a compromise between two contending idioms; the Germanic conqueror learnt the language of the conquered, Gaul, lopped off, without any consideration, all inflexions which he found cumbersome, and was thus forced to submit to a definite rule the sequence of words in sentences which till then had been quite free; besides, he grafted on the dry Latin stock numerous new and vigorous expressions borrowed from his native German. Up to the sixteenth century traces of Germanic vigour remained alive. Montaigne still indulged in the liberty of forming and composing words; but he did not prevail, and shortly after him the flame died out for ever.

A much stronger force lives in the English language; it alone possesses qualities capable of making it a dangerous rival of the German. Here the conditions are just the opposite of the French; the Norman Conqueror had already succumbed to the French language; the Anglo-Saxon, beaten on the field, but numerically the stronger, possessed the more vigorous language. From this composition, in which the Teutonic element retained the upper hand—particularly in respect to the general structure of the language—a marvellous medium of human intercourse has developed, so that a Shakespeare could arise from its midst and shed forth light.

And yet! As soon as we look more closely we discover a terrible and irreparable blemish. English is capable of serving as a vehicle for the sublime, the phantastic as well as for the energetic, the political debate, for all that is direct, thus also for business, sport, for the trivial and the brutal; but it is impossible to reveal thoughts of delicacy and depth in English. Even the thoughts of brilliant thinkers are stunted and parched, and half Scottish Kant had to be born in Germany, so that he might complete the work begun by his countryman

Hume. The reason is this: for all higher mental activity words of Latin-French origin only are employed; the nobleman alone had leisure to think; the Saxon populace that had become serfs was occupied with hard work and could, at the most, find time for poetry in the evening when toil was done. Thus, when the time came for new modes of thought there was no tractable material, only clumsy, rusty armour.

Consequently England remained excluded from the highest attainments of the last two centuries, as it could not participate in the conscious and unconscious mental life of Germany, which was leading in the world; thence a daily increasing leeway, which had long become evident to the more clear-sighted. For by thought I by no means mean, in the first place, philosophy, but the most valuable part of science and art as well as of all that contributes to culture and to the formation of a scientific point of view, to a life of mental activity. English natural science, for instance, is for the uneducated man an entirely incomprehensible rigmarole, composed of nothing but barbaric Latin and Greek words, interspersed with still less comprehensible and unpronounceable German technical terms—it is a technical achievement and not a means of culture. An English theologian—to take another example—who is ignorant of German, no longer knows what are the questions of the day in this science. This is the reason why not a single ray of real enlightenment ever penetrates to the people; there is no language by the medium of which it might find its way. Fichte's words: "In a people with a living tongue culture penetrates daily life, where this is not the case culture and life take each its own separate course," may be applied to a comparison between the German and the English language. The very high, aristocratic, liberal culture to be found in England stands completely outside the pale of national life; it has not the slightest influence on the attitude of the people, on the ruling classes, on the aims and means of the state.

Hence the absolute necessity that the German language—not the English—should become the universal language. Should English come off victorious, human culture is cut off, dedicated to death. The moral corruption of England has revealed itself since the commencement of the present war in the most terrible manner; mendacity, brutality, violence, boasting, at the same time a complete lack of dignity, justice, virility, truly a sad spectacle. Let the immense colonial possessions and other countries of English tongue get into a position to expose their thoughts and souls, and with horror it will be revealed what brutality is hidden here, the final phase of brutality in the human race. Therefore the German—and with him the German language—must be victorious. And when once he has gained the victory—be it to-day or in a hundred years—the necessity remains the same—then there will be no more important task than to enforce the German language on the world. Everywhere, even among foreign races, there are, among hundreds of thousands, men of great talents and of noble mind; without a knowledge of German they remain excluded from the highest range of culture. Nor do I only think of men of genius, on all, particularly on the simple, the humble, those who stand closest to nature, the German language acts as a blessing sent straight from the hand of God into the human heart. What language contains "tales" like those collected by the brothers Grimm? And, although Shakespeare, who, by the way, lives only in Germany and not in England, is always being cast up to us, does not the German language possess in Luther an incomparable treasure, an inexhaustible source of popular eloquence, flowing besides from a heroic genius? Why was the Reformation never a success in England, in Poland, and in France? Because only the German language possessed the strength to overcome the foreign element in Christianity. I do not say this to annoy German Roman Catholics, let them remain faithful to their creed; but we all became Germans through Luther's work. He taught us to see in the German people, in German politics, divine institutions worthy of love and veneration. Thus he laid the foundation. And from then on—I mean from the moment when the German soul revealed itself in folk-lore tales and its natural vigour in this strong man—the divine "thought" of the German language rises to the great creator of thoughts and words in which new ideas gain form and live—to Immanuel Kant, whom none can fathom who do not know German—it rises to Goethe, the sublime counterpart of Kant, of whom Jacob Grimm so rightly says: "Without him we can hardly imagine ourselves Germans," so strong is this mystic power of native language and poetry. It rises to the high summit where German music—the art that stormed the heavens—united so completely with the German language that from this moment the latter became capable of expressing the inexpressible, and thus humanity received in works of art a new organ which is inseparable from the German language, as word and sound form but a single unity.

This dream of the universal German language is practicable; it is not only in the interest of the Germans, it is their duty. This duty contains two commands. Firstly: no German must ever abandon his language, neither he nor his children's children. Secondly: in every place and at every time he should endeavour to enforce it on others, till everywhere it triumphs like the arms of our national armies. Let the business man lead the way and demand German from his correspondents, as has been done up to now by the English and Americans in regard to their language. By extension of colonial empire and increase of the mercantile marine the German language will go with the German flag to all quarters of the world, and no longer as an inferior idiom begging for sufferance and decked with disjointed scraps of English, but everywhere regarded as the language of efficiency, honesty, and enlightenment, and, therefore the most esteemed.

As far as the Empire extends let the clergymen teach and preach only in German, the teacher instruct in no other tongue. Abroad, let no German commit the crime of abandoning his language. Let him learn to understand that in so doing he renders himself guilty of a disgraceful deed. If all Germans in the United States, in Canada, Australia, etc., faithfully retain their language throughout generations, then the day will soon come when this language will claim equal rights in legislative bodies and government departments, and when this is attained it will penetrate victoriously into the life of the continents. In the meanwhile, schools must do their uttermost that German become the language of all higher education. It must be rendered clear that he who does not know German is a pariah. Foreign nations will learn German forced by envy, avarice, duty, ambition. All causes are the same to me; with the German language we make everyone an inestimable gift, and we need have no compunction as to the means by which we force it on him.

It is thus that I image the victorious course of the German language; and should I no longer experience it, the present war leads me to hope that, perhaps, I shall not close my eyes without seeing the beginning of the realisation of the most fervent of all the wishes of my heart. You see, there is a subjective tinge in the confidence of which I spoke above, a subjective tinge: As I believe in God, so I believe in the holy German language!

IV.

GERMANY AS LEADING POWER IN THE WORLD.

IV.

GERMANY AS LEADING POWER IN THE WORLD.

A FRIEND of mine—a German—is asking himself and therefore also me, in evident anxiety, if a victorious Germany would possess the political maturity which would render it capable of becoming the leading power in the world. I am deeply touched that, in the midst of the joy of victory, a man should put this anxious question to his soul; this is true German. If many think thus, then we may look with confidence towards the coming days of peace. At all events, the question deserves an answer. I will give mine in the few following lines.

It is not easy at the present time to remain calm, to observe calmly, judge calmly, speak calmly. And yet it is dangerous not to do so. For things of heavy import are not produced in excitement, but by clear-sightedness, reflection, energy. The German victories are not, in the first place, due to the "furor teutonicus" of which one hears so much; on the contrary, they are mainly based on the calm, efficient, and foreseeing work of decades. By well-informed quarters I am told the whole of the present plan of campaign dates in its very details back to old Moltke; he had drawn up a plan for a war on two as well as on three fronts. This plan has been kept up-to-date by the indefatigable labours of the General Staff—new means of transport, auto-transport, aeronautics, the new arms have all been taken into consideration, and the plan extended; in addition it has been nearly daily tested as to its readiness. Thus we had first the deed of the genius and then the never relaxing difficult application to duty of the many. And only then, finally, the third factor—which in reality lay as an element at the bottom of the other two—the usually hidden vigour of the nation, a greatness of ideal reality which unites the mental ardour of the genius with the implicit sacrifice of obedience. We see, in order that a nation may accomplish really great things, three factors must unite: thorough efficiency of the nation as a whole; great talents in individuals; a methodical training of many. Yet it is evident that the simple existence of these forces is of no avail, if they do not work together in such a manner that each attains its full result.

But here we are laying our hand on the sore place in the political state of Germany to-day. As in no other country in the world all that is necessary exists to attain in this sphere also the greatest of results; but the different parts do not work in union; waste of strength, waste of time, waste of men. Of what use would a Moltke have been if he had been sent "planter ses choux" in some provincial town? Thus the most capable men of Germany are allowed to decay. What could a nation attain that never had a chance of revealing itself as "spontaneous force," but must submit for years to be lectured by pettifogging lawyers and pot-house politicians on things which it does not understand, to be broken up into twenty parties who are constantly at one another's throat. How magnificently great, yes, let us say it, how holy great, does the German nation appear as soon as the above-mentioned elements work together. Ah, happy we, to-day we once more experience it! Every belief bursts forth again, every hope, even the most forlorn, seems to find justification. We see that the impossible is possible. As in the army, so in the work of peace, there is nothing which Germany could not attain. And what a glorious prospect for the future of humanity to be placed under the influence of such a Germany. And yet many men are unable to feel confident in this respect. The difference between military Germany and political Germany is too marked.

Of the forces which give their power to military Germany only the second comes into play in political matters. All respect for German officials! And yet into what a groove of disappointment and sourness they have got. Officials like the German ones, scientifically and methodically trained for the highest functions, require internal liberty to carry out with joy their duty, and this can only be given them by tasks which appeal to their genius, and the execution of which demands that they employ all their faculties. The official, if great things are to be attained, should be in a similar position to the officer in times of war, raised up by wings from above with firm support below. For this, new ways would have to be prescribed by the hand of a genius, and boldly and calmly entered on. New ideals cannot be attained by old ways. The organisation of the German army was at first an idea in the brain of an individual man before, in the course of a century, it became that which causes our astonishment and admiration to-day; and because it was an idea, thousands have joyfully collaborated at its realisation.

The German national vigour should not become a parody of itself in the unbearably trivial form of the German Reichstag. What a satire on the tragic events of 1914 is the Zabern debate which preceded them and ended with the disgraceful and, at the same time, ridiculous vote of censure! It will be said that the Reichstag has now behaved well! That is not so. It was the whole German people that rose as one man in their unique greatness. No Reichstag could oppose this mighty movement; not members of the Reichstag, but Germans seized the Kaiser's hand; as German men they acted in the only possible way. But the Reichstag reassembled, and at once the old trouble recommenced; everything was delayed, everything suffocated, and political life resembled a Trojan field of ruins. If Germany desires, as a political power, the same success as a military power, radical changes must be carried out; and for new wants new forms and new methods be found and invented. To tell the truth, all nations of the earth are sick and tired of parliaments; tired of the sacred general franchise; tired of the ever-running flow of oratory, which threatens to drown the whole of the civilised world, as in a new Deluge. Silence is strength. Ask General Quartermaster von Stein if I am not right. Chattering leads to complete imbecility. That will be the result of present-day parliaments. And if I am asked what position the people are to occupy in the arrangement of the new political whole, my answer is:

The people will be the unconscious root, supplying nutriment, the reserve of forces, and will then prove themselves as efficient as now in the German army. As soon as the people are brought to silence, their voice is most distinctly heard. Their speech is not dialectic, but something which far surpasses it. A monarch may be represented, a class, a profession—a people cannot be represented. The people are nature, and a Mr. Müller or Mr. Meyer is as little able to represent them as he is to represent a mountain or a wood. This pretended representation of the people does nothing but destroy the real vigour of the people and cause a chaos. It causes incessant restlessness and, therefore, anxiety. It consumes every root fibre which would have served to sustain life. It stultifies by its debate and nullifies all great plans by its disputes. In addition to this, like a monstrous dragon, it swallows mountains of strength and oceans of time, all of which are lost for ever for the life of the nation. The people naturally recognise and foster great characters; parliament invariably refuses to tolerate any talent that arises above mediocrity. Read Bismarck's speeches and then read the speeches in which the "High House" replied. It is a school of disgust! However, it is a good sign that, among all the parliaments of the world, the German "Reichstag" must be regarded as the most unbearable. From this we see how un-German this inheritance of the French Revolution is. It is true the French Chamber is slowly ruining the country, but more "esprit" and wit are shown there than in the German Reichstag; to bandy words so that assertion and retort fly like a ball from one to the other suits the French character better, as well as the spectacular nature of the prearranged debates to which spectators of both sex press as to a theatre. All this in nowise suits the German character.

The English Parliament is also rapidly approaching a catastrophe since the days when it ceased to be an assembly of landed proprietors and intellectual capacities to become the hunting-ground of political attorneys. Yet there still exist in it great traditions of real Germanic worth which endow it with a dignity which the German Reichstag lacks entirely.

No nation is nearly so rich in manifold political institutions as Germany. Truly she has no need to borrow forms of government from abroad. How dead is France with her single town where politicians, artists, scholars, and cocottes all live one upon the top of the other, all round surrounded by 500,000 square kilometres of philistines without art, without science, without society, "agri deserti" as far as intellectual life is concerned.

What an unformly, monstrous chaos Russia represents, a conglomerate held together only by the law of indolence! What a weak ideal is beautiful Austria united solely by its loyalty to the House of Hapsburg, but otherwise all parts striving asunder in hostile antipathy. And how deep has England sunk since she abandoned her inherited aristocratic principles of government for the gain of money.

But in Germany every spot is alive, because

here manifold historical traditions live and work, because here alone the present grows out of the past. The kingdoms, duchies, free towns, the democratic and aristocratic forms of government, all exhale a life such as has never been seen before. For God's sake no unifying, no uniformity. Germany is a real, organic unity, because it consists of parts. The present German Empire is an entirely new formation in the history of mankind, therefore it can, shall, and must produce new forms of political life. Away with English and French patterns!

No less must Germany adopt new ways in the conception of her relations to other states. Here Bismarck has shown us the way. Instead of accepted "diplomacy" he showed how to practise statesmancraft, a new, real German statesmancraft, wary but not mendacious, clever but not Machiavellian, daring to foolhardiness; but, in truth, as well thought out and cautious as a campaign plan of the German General Staff.

After Bismarck's, unfortunately, too early departure, Germany immediately strayed again on foreign paths. No attention was paid to the fundamental truth that a statesman may occasionally be an excellent diplomatist (*vide* Bismarck in Petrograd and Paris), but an ordinary diplomatist never has the makings of a real statesman. No worse misfortune could happen to Germany than once more to come under Metternich's principles of government. Let it not be said history knows but one Bismarck; principles work with might when once they have been recognised and boldly seized; they show the way and produce men; exactly as in war, all at once, generals arise whose genius, in times of peace, no one would have suspected.

No, there is no lack of the right men in Germany, only room must be made for them. Therefore, above all, away with the old school of diplomatists. There is not a German who within the bounds of real "diplomacy" is capable of contending with the Greys,

Delclassés, Iswolskis, or whatever their names may be. The best feature of post-Bismarckean time was that men were sent to the most dangerous posts who by nature of their character and intelligence could not be led into dark, tortuous ways. Thus, at least, a German trait was preserved in the midst of all this un-German business. But now things must become different, otherwise political Germany will succumb in spite of all the victories of military Germany. For God's sake, no more Ambassadors' Conferences!

When once Germany has gained the power—and that she will gain it we all most confidently expect—she must at once set about instituting the scientific policy of genius. Exactly as Augustus undertook a reformation of the world, so Germany must do it now. A great policy can only be thought out by a few and carried out with iron consequence. It is absurd to think that a whole people can carry out a policy. There is much talk of the people nowadays, but, after all, in the last instance, it is always certain classes who gain possession of the power and use it for their own selfish ends. Germany must not become an industrial, nor a financial, nor an agricultural state. It must be governed by a class which stands outside the parties and spheres of special interest. These are the sole conditions of a scientific policy of genius. All this may sound Utopic, but a new era demands new methods. The fact should not be overlooked that, although Germany is now victorious in Europe, that is not an end to the struggle. The inhabitants of other continents are there. The ultimate victory will be with him who judges the problems as Moltke judged the possible eventualities of the war, and who, like the German General Staff, strong, conscious, faithful, and *above all* without having to submit to any interference by lawyers representing, or rather misrepresenting, the people, carries out the firmly drawn up plan.

For the new time new aims and new means!

V.

ENGLAND

V.

ENGLAND.

An old experience teaches us: Anyone who has spent six weeks in a foreign country sits down boldly and writes a bright book describing clearly and briefly with astonishing simplicity the national character, the customs, qualities, and failings of a people, so that he who runs may read, as the English say. He who has spent six months in conscientious observation writes with much greater caution; his book runs the risk of wearying the reader, who wishes to acquire definite knowledge and now gropes in uncertainties, due to reservations and indefinite statements. But he who has lived there six years and had the opportunity of coming into close contact with a number of differently constituted individuals of the nation in question, so that he has been able to observe in their minds the effect of events in action and reaction, and has gained knowledge not only of their character, but of the peculiar trend of their character—he will abandon the intention of writing a book on that nation, because he cannot hope to do justice to so complicated a subject into which it is so difficult to gain an insight. It is a different matter when a man who himself belongs to this people, and therefore possesses an inexhaustible and inexhaustive knowledge of them, lets the past which also is well known to him pass before his mind's eye; he gains deep insights at certain points; it is there where character and history clash. Suddenly, he then becomes aware that this character, if the course of historic events had not forced upon it just this definite line of development, must have turned out quite different, and that the same historic course would certainly have had quite a different effect on a character moulded on other lines. One must proceed with the utmost caution as soon as one speaks of the "character" of a nation; for, as it is necessarily composed of innumerable, different, individual characters, one runs the risk of producing a picture in the manner of Lombroso, who had the faces of fifty murderers photographed one above the other in order to attain the physiognomy of the ideal murderer, by which means a perfectly characterless type was produced, the only certain quality of which was that it certainly did not resemble any murderer who had ever lived.

But with a nation the blood relationship which penetrates everywhere does much to unify, and much is also contributed by the "psyche" of the masses, *i.e.*, the influence to which the individual is subjected by those around him. Thus, for instance, the unity of the German national character is revealed with overwhelming force at the present moment; 1914 is for Germany one of those moments when history and character clash; suddenly we gain an insight right into the interior, which is otherwise hidden from the eye by the deceptive surface.

In the same manner and at the same moment—not with the same unity, let us hope to God, but yet distinctly and decisively—a clash between English character and English history is revealed. And we stand before it overwhelmed with horror and shame. For it is of no avail that journalists maintain that the English are no longer Teutons, and that they prove it by their conduct; they are Teutons, much purer Teutons than many Germans, and the development of the last two centuries has placed the Anglo-Saxon element, *i.e.*, the real Teuton element, more and more in the foreground at the expense of the Norman-French element, which is constantly losing ground by intermarrying. The influence of the Jews cannot be asserted, although it is particularly great in the present government. Germany has twenty times as many Jews, where are they now? As if blown away by the mighty rising, as "Jews" no longer to be found; for they are doing their duty as Germans at the front or at home. Whereas the English Jews, who are the natural brothers and cousins of the German Jews, participate in all the disgraceful actions there, hastily change their German names into English ones, and, in the Press, of which they have gained almost complete possession, lead the campaign of slander against Germany. If a nation rises, the Jew follows. He does not lead. The causes of the development which has placed England where she now stands are to be sought much deeper, in the events of past centuries. This was one of the possible developments of the Germanic race; from the disharmony between history and character it has become a fact. If one reflects on the history of states, one is more and more astonished at the far-reaching effect, which spreads by channels no eye can overlook, of simple events and of hardly perceptible turns of fate. It is sufficient to bear in mind one single event at the commencement of English history, and a single turn caused by external circumstances which took place five hundred years later, to understand many things which would otherwise remain an unsolvable enigma. From these two facts there results—as effect—a third. From the peculiarly constituted effect arises necessarily a just as peculiar counteraction, and thus, ultimately—as with all organic life—an infinitely manifold and individual whole is composed of the most simple components imaginable, in which all parts are interdependent. The conquest by the Normans, which, in the eleventh century, subjected the Anglo-Saxon population, is the "event" which I have in my mind; the "turn of fate" is the process, beginning about the sixteenth century, by which the agricultural inhabitants of England, in spite of their innate dread of the sea, were turned into mariners and merchants. There can be no doubt that distinctive and, for a foreigner, inexplicable traits of character in the English nation are derived, in the first place, from a conjunction of the Saxon forms of government, which already, under Alfred the Great, had attained a very high standard, with the spirit of the vigorous Norman; just as little can it be doubted that from the moment when the change to a commercial nation took place, a change commenced in the whole political community, which ultimately was bound to lead to the catastrophe, the commencement of which we see to-day.

By "nobility" something quite different is understood in England to what the term conveys in other countries. It is not a question of a title by which all members of the family are externally distinguished for all times; but of belonging to a social caste, which forms a distinct internal contrast to the rest of the people. Incessantly people fall out of this caste, incessantly others are received into it by assimilation. Every Englishman who belongs to the "nobility" or "gentry" is to be known at once; very frequently by his features, always by the expression of his face, by his behaviour, by his voice, and, above all things, with absolute certainty by his speech. No importance is attached to the title, which is only given to one of the contemporaries of the family; all importance is attached to the caste. Aristocratic men often refuse titles. Some of the leading families have refused titles of nobility for centuries. To compare this with the French ancient régime would be erroneous. It is true the Frank, the Burgundian, and the Gothic nobility could be distinctly distinguished from the other people up to the Revolution; at present their imposing physiognomies are very rarely seen in France. In England the conditions were quite different from the very beginning, and the nobility have assumed a position of far greater importance. The Burgundians, Franks, and Goths penetrated as whole nations into Gaul; the greater part was entirely assimilated by the original inhabitants; only princes and nobles held aloof, and they were not numerous enough to maintain their position long. On the other hand, the number of noble families who followed the first kings from Normandy and Anjou to England was relatively small, so that this nobility, which received and assimilated only a few Saxon and Danish families, remained completely separated from the people, who retained their unalloyed Anglo-Saxon blood. Hence the fact of this upper caste which is distinctive of England, a caste which, up to the present day, possesses its own language, or, to be more exact, its own pronunciation; but this pronunciation includes numerous words and idioms which an Englishman who does not belong to this caste is as incapable of using correctly as he is of attaining the pronunciation. By this circumstance the nation was divided into two parts, and has remained so to the present day: an upper and a lower; an aristocratic and a plebeian. William the Conqueror endeavoured, but without success, to learn Anglo-Saxon. The great historian, Hobbes, tells us that under the early Norman kings those who complained of the tyranny of the new nobility received as answer: "Silence, thou art but an Englishman." And yet this simple Englishman came off victorious by persistently refusing to learn French. In the same manner—and this is the critical point—the upper caste refused to learn Anglo-Saxon. The new language was the result of this twofold obstinacy, it is called English; it arose from two contending idioms, each of which desired prevalence for itself, but even after the definite settlement the contest continued in the two pronunciations of the present time, the aristocratic and the common.

He who bears in mind this circumstance,

the language, will soon, even without a personal acquaintance with England, procure a deeper insight into many matters than extensive works on the subject could have provided. Thus it comes that secondary schools open to the whole nation, as they exist everywhere, in Germany, France, Italy, etc., are impossible in England. "I cannot send my son to a school," says the aristocratic Englishman, "where he would learn from comrades and masters the pronunciation ''igh' for 'high,' and 'hisland' for 'island.'" Besides, there is the ugly nasal pronunciation which has developed in the towns in England and, to a much greater extent, in America and Australia. The German "Gymnasium" and "Realschule" are impossible; there are institutions for the education of the sons of the aristocracy and for those of the lower class; the boys never get to know one another, do not speak to one another, and despise each other. Therefore a university, in the German sense, is impossible. The ancient universities are exclusively aristocratic, and produce those exquisite English scholars who, secluded from common life, live in their mediæval colleges, men of great experience in life and society, as is natural for the ruling class of a ruling nation, frequently with the necessary leisure for study and travel; they represent in their personality and books the highest grade of culture which, at the present day, can be attained by humanity. It is true, they are the product of a hot-house.

But the new universities are mainly technical schools. Some eminent professors —particularly of chemistry, physics, mechanics—who have all acquired their knowledge in Germany, teach at them, but they have no influence on the character of the institutions, which is exclusively practical and in no sense addicted to pure science.

One of the main supports of modern Germany is thus entirely lacking in England: the influence of school and university which penetrate the life of the nation by a thousand veins and raise it to a unity of culture.

No less does England lack the possibility of a national army, of that powerful, moral creation which one might call the backbone of modern Germany. For the German army would not possess its enormous moral power if the absolute unity of all forces of the nation were not united and reflected in it. From Imperial Majesty to the youngest peasant recruit they all form one single family, each one a comrade to the other, all united by obedience, duty, patriotism. Before the army could develop and bring the unity of Germany to its highest power, the moral and mental unity to desire and create such an army had to exist. This is wanting in England. In England the two classes of the people—the small and the large—know nothing of one another, absolutely nothing. I can have a servant for twenty years and know as little about him as about the soul of my walking-stick. The pride of the Englishman who does not belong to the upper caste is his unapproachability. He does not wish to be questioned; he does not wish to speak; he does not say "Good morning"; he does not say "Good night"; if he meets his master, he goes out of his way so as not to have to salute. What comradeship can then exist between soldier and officer? How is unity to be attained? The relationship is and remains that of the aristocrat, who gives orders to men belonging to a different class and enforces obedience by his innate superiority.

Besides, the English of the lower classes have from the beginning been unwarlike. The Plantagenets waged many wars in France and distinguished themselves in the Holy Land; but with the exception of the nobility they drew no soldiers from England. Green, the well-known historian, writes: "The inhabitants of England took no interest in wars and crusades, what they valued in their kings was that they procured lasting peace for the island." And that has remained so up to the present day when the English army is composed to the much greater part of Celtic Irish and Celtic Scotch. The real English do not enlist. In the English battles of the past Englishmen of the nobility have commanded, but the armies consisted of foreign levies, mostly Germans. The battles in India have, from the commencement, been principally fought with Indian troops, and not with English; the legal percentage was one-fifth Englishmen, and these "Englishmen" were mostly Irish. The excellent descriptions of recruiting which we find in Shakespeare are known to every educated German, from *Henry IV.*, Part II. An amusing confirmation is to be found in the letters of the Venetian ambassador about the same time. At the commencement of 1617 England wished to assist the Republic against Spain. The Doge accepted the services of a Scottish count bringing soldiers from Scotland and Ireland, but he refused the

English auxiliaries, saying: "He had no great opinion of them and knew how much their ardour depended on the three B's—Beef, Beer, and Bed." Then look up von Noorden's "War of the Spanish Succession." You will find that in 1708 England had to make up her mind to legislate against the lack of English recruits, which was increasing year by year. It is the same story 1200, 1600, 1700, and 1900. I could quote dozens of examples. The insular situation is no sufficient explanation. Before our eyes we see how the Island Empire of Japan has raised a formidable national army. I am persuaded the real cause lies in the "event," the mixing of the races, followed by the social disruption and augmented by the "turn of fate," of which I shall speak soon.

It may be added that the theory England did not need a large army, and ought not to maintain one, served as a support to the practice at an early date. No statesman was ever more respected by his countrymen than

Lord Bolingbroke. Far beyond his life he remained the prophet of the peculiar lines of development of modern England. In the midst of the victories of Queen Anne, Bolingbroke, in his "Observations on the History of England," explains England should have a large fleet, but not a standing army, for the latter "would approach England too much to the Continent," whereas it was England's interest to let the continental powers wage war upon each other "without, herself, becoming too deeply involved." An army would entail "great economical inconveniences and, at the same time, serious dangers."

A third thing should be shortly mentioned. The whole legislation of England—the state, the constitution, her policy—is in the hands of a single class of society without any real assistance from the other. Hobbes frankly confesses it: "Parliament has never represented the whole nation." The Reformation would have been the touchstone, for everywhere religion is the most internal wheel of politics. And what do we find? Those Englishmen who really broke loose from Rome soon had to flee their country and seek liberty of conscience in the deserts of North America; whereas the separation of the Established Church took place as a purely political measure of the very absolute King, Henry VIII., nearly without consulting Parliament. The inhabitants of England went to bed as Roman Catholics and awoke the next morning as Anglicans. The talk about English political liberty has always irritated me; from the commencement of history it has only been the question of the liberty of a caste. Athens had "leisure" to be free, because the 20,000 free citizens were served by 400,000 slaves; England could allow herself the luxury of a so-called free Parliament, because this Parliament was entirely in the hands of rich men, who derived pleasure and power from governing. Thomas de Quincey, an author much too little known in Germany, one of the richest talents England ever produced, shows that the extension of the influence and rights of the Lower House since about 1600 are by no means to be attributed to an increase of the strength of the people, but to the increase of the lower nobility, that is to say, of the families descended from younger sons; these have, by degrees, pushed aside the hereditary nobility and the bishops. It was very wise of the Parliament to obtain rights for the people; it strengthened it against the king, and gave it the power to execute him who refused to submit to the dictates of the ruling caste; but with no less sanguinary means it has contrived to suppress every attempt of the people to gain real power. Even to-day, when the franchise is extended so as to include a considerable proportion of the non-aristocratic people, the old violence of the governing class may still be seen. Many readers will know Dickens's description of a parliamentary election in the "Pickwick Papers."

I can confirm them myself from a later period. On the day of the election, a special train brought four hundred roughs into the little provincial town from the nearest industrial centre. They were the hired guard of the conservative party. These men were in no way interested in the election in a strange town; they were there to inspire awe in the liberal voters and—if not successful in this—to break their skulls. Fortunately, the liberal committee had not been remiss, and shortly afterwards three hundred still more ugly roughs arrived from another part of the country. The whole day there was shouting, fighting; voters were hauled out of their carriages by the feet; orators pelted with rotten eggs, etc.—a peculiar conception of the liberty of political opinion and the free right to vote. In the evening I experienced it on my own person—for, at that time, I was a pupil in a college, and of the eighty inhabitants of my "house" the only one who wore the liberal badge, thus confessing himself an adherent of Gladstone's. Not even the prayers of the masters prevailed upon me to lay aside the colours of my convictions and replace them by those of Disraeli, and so the whole pack fell upon me, knocked me down, and beat me, till the masters and servants hastened to my assistance. On that day—it is now forty-six years ago—I learnt more about the English constitution and the English conception of liberty than later from the books of Hallam and Gneist. In English politics two uncultured forces are opposed, supplementing each other: the uncultured violence of the class accustomed to rule, and the elementary lack of culture of the entirely ignorant masses, who, as was shown above, never have an opportunity of getting into touch with higher civilisation.

All these peculiarities date back to the event which as a sudden *coup de main* in 1066 put an end to the fine civilisation of the Anglo-Saxon state and created the kingdom of England. In my opinion, the roots both of England's rise and fall are to be found here.

But now for the curious "turn of fate," for without it the general demoralisation of all classes which we have to deplore would never have come about.

John Robert Seeley, in his classic book, "The Expansion of England," has long ago exposed the legend that the English were naturally bold mariners, like the Vikings of the early Normans. The contrary is true. It has been very difficult to imbue them with a taste for the sea. Seeley, at the same time, points out that the English are, in reality, by no means conquerors. They have founded colonies where the countries were uninhabited or only inhabited by naked savages—others they have swindled from the Dutch, the French, the Spanish, by treaties, or, as in the case of Malta, by breach of treaty. India was subjected by Indian troops. Never has England undertaken conquests by force of arms as the French and the Spaniards have done. The English do not wage war like Alexander or Cæsar, for the sake of glory. "For England," says Seeley, "war is an industry, one of the possible ways of becoming rich, the best business, the most profitable investment." This may be laudable or not; I only mention it because this trait is a supplement to the others. The fact is that the English are not soldiers, and not bold, daring mariners, but were solely enticed on the water by trade. Trade in peace, trade by means of war; army and navy, but not for the unity and power of the country, but for the advancement of wealth in all parts of the world, certainly honest and brave, but not the expression of a national need, a national idea.

Naturally, the insular position always rendered it necessary that England should receive many commodities from across the water; not only conquerors, but merchandise of all kinds came from there. For many centuries this trade was in foreign hands. Under the successors of William I. it was the French of Normandy and Picardy who monopolised the English trade; then particularly the German Hansa, and later on the so-called Flemish Hansa; Venice and Genoa conducted, according to special treaties, the whole of the commerce to and from the Mediterranean, without the intervention of English ships. Even the fishing along the English coasts was chiefly carried out by the Dutch, so that when Henry VIII. made the timid attempt to foster the first society of Merchant Adventurers, and tried to found a navy for its protection, he experienced the greatest difficulty in procuring the sailors necessary to man it. To overcome this difficulty a law was made under his successor, Edward VI., in 1549, forcing the English to eat fish on Fridays and Saturdays, as well as during Lent and on all days of atonement, under penalty of a fine. Elizabeth was careful to enforce this measure and to do all in her power to encourage fishing. At a time, therefore, when the Italians, Spaniards, and Portuguese had already produced generations of bold, ingenious ocean seamen, laws were necessary to drive the English to catch herrings and flounders off their own coasts (*vide* Cunningham, "Growth of English Industry and Commerce"). Now things certainly advanced quickly, and the same Doge who refused English troops was very pleased to accept the help of English fighting ships, which, although only armed merchantmen, were reckoned as belonging to the Royal Navy.

In July, 1518, for the very first time in history, seven English men-of-war sailed into the Mediterranean, as a modest contribution to a powerful Dutch and Venetian fleet (Corbett, "England in the Mediterranean"). Now England had recognised the new position of things in the world, and the opportunity which it offered of acquiring wealth. All problematic questions had already been settled by others; the East and West Passage had been discovered, the New World opened up, India rendered accessible, communications established with China; now was the time to seize what was to be had according to the moral of Mephistopheles:

> "The question's what, and by no means why?
> I needs be ignorant of navigation;
> War, commerce, and free piracy
> Form but one trinity, no separation."

Here the new point at which England's policy commences is clearly indicated: war, commerce, and piracy.

As soon as England embarks on foreign trade she begins to hate; first of all the German Hansa. Those who wish to know more about the subject need only look up Schanz's "England's Commercial Policy." Immediately piracy commences; without declaring war, England attacks Jamaica, which belonged to Spain, and lays the foundation to her West Indian Empire. For a long time England's colonial activity is restricted to capturing the Spanish galleons as they return home laden with gold and precious wares. Everywhere commercial England grows at the expense of other nations, and increases by their destruction. Piracy precedes, through it commerce prospers; wars are waged when there is no other resource, but Lord Bolingbroke's "island policy" is never forgotten. First England unites with Holland to destroy the colonial empire of the Spanish; then with France to sever the vital nerve of Holland; then she perceives how ingeniously the great Frenchman Dupleix has attacked the Indian problem, imitates him, and incites the natives against him, then the natives against each other, till ultimately, as Seeley says, "without conquest" she acquires one of the largest empires in the world. On the threshold of the nineteenth century, Kant, the mildest, but one of the most clear-sighted of men, describes

England as "the most bellicose and most prone to violence of all states." How abjectly immoral the people soon became under the influence of this new spirit may be shown by a single example: how they glory in English schools in the battles won by Marlborough with his German soldiers! What now was their real aim and result? To assure for England the monopoly of the slave trade! Lecky, the author of the great "History of England in the Eighteenth Century," says after the peace of Utrecht (1713) the slave trade formed "the centre of the whole English policy." As long as this trade remained profitable the English carried it on. Liverpool, for instance, has not grown great by its industry, but through the tracking down and bartering of millions of unhappy negroes. The patriotic historian Green says verbally: "The terrible cruelties and iniquities of this trade, the ruin of Africa, and the annihilation of human dignity did not arouse sympathy in a single Englishman."

Then Green proceeds to the description of the endeavours of individual philanthropists. But for decades these were of no avail. Parliament was deaf. The merchants were furious—until the day when a new position caused this trade to be no longer desirable, and now amidst disgusting, hypocritical protests of humanity and England's mission to hold up a light to all nations of the world, etc., the slave trade is prohibited by law.

We are fortunate enough to possess Goethe's clear and lasting judgment on this subject: "Everyone knows the protestations of the English against the slave trade, and whilst they attempt to prove to us what humane principles underlie their action, it is now discovered that the true motive is a mercenary aim, without which the English, as is well known, never undertake anything. On the west coast of Africa they now require the negroes in their large possessions, and it is contrary to their interests to export them from there. In America they have established large colonies of negroes which are profitable, and yearly produce a large quantity of negroes. With these they cover their North-American demand, and, as in this manner, they carry on a very profitable trade, an import from abroad would be injurious to their commercial interest, and they, therefore, proclaim, not without an object, against this inhuman traffic."

It is impossible, and also unnecessary, to describe how the exclusive addiction to trade and industry, to the acquirement of money, gradually caused the destruction of England's agriculture. At the turn of the eighteenth to nineteenth century the English weavers lived in comfortable cottages in the country, surrounded by vegetable gardens and fields. To-day only a very rich merchant can afford to live in the country in England, for the cultivation of the ground does not cover the expenses. In the year 1769, of a census of eight and a half millions,

2,800,000 were employed in agricultural labour and tending cattle; in 1897, with a population of forty millions, only 798,000 men and women were employed on the land (Gibbons, "The Industrial History of England," 4th edition).

With this a deeply penetrating change of the whole character of both classes is closely connected; by this development the life and soul of the Englishman has been completely altered. Old England had for centuries enjoyed the inestimable good fortune of not having to dread an external enemy, and she had waged her few wars with foreign soldiers. Thus agriculture and country life were blessed with great prosperity, and as the old poets tell us, and the new scholars prove by statistics, not only the lords, but also the small holders and labourers, were incomparably better off than now. England enjoyed throughout Europe a reputation for comfort and merriment.

A traveller of the fifteenth century observes

that the English seem "less troubled with hard work than other people, and are able to lead a more refined life and give more time to intellectual pursuits." Another speaks of their incomparable kindness. All this has changed.

To intellectual pursuits in present-day England I have referred in the "Essay on German Liberty," page 55; but in regard to "merry old England," that flourished most at the time of Henry VIII. and Elizabeth, and is known to us all from Shakespeare and Walter Scott, and which we all love, it has disappeared entirely, at first gradually and then with surprising rapidity in inverse ratio with the development of shipping and industry. In the novels of the eighteenth century, it is still to be seen like the uncanny glare of a sultry sunset. The genius of Dickens still shows it us in the hearts of some whimsical characters, where, hovering between caricature and melancholy insight into their own unreal existence, it passes on to definite decease. To-day the last vestige has been trampled down. No comfort is to be found in England, no broad and kindly humour, no merriment. Everything, as far as public life is concerned, is haste, money, noise, show, vulgarity, arrogance, discouragement, and envy. One remembers the beautiful old English Christmas festival with red-berried holly and the mistletoe, beneath which innocent kisses were stolen. On this day least of all, even thirty years ago, no one could have been enticed away from his home. To-day the dining-rooms of all the immense hotels of London are sold out weeks before; they sit at a thousand tables, family by family, eat and drink until, at midnight, the singing of trivial street-songs in the style of the disgusting "For he's a jolly good fellow" begins, after which the tables are quickly cleared and all the young men and girls, who are entirely unknown to each other, devote themselves in disgusting promiscuity to the execution of negro dances, whilst the older elements gamble in the card-rooms. It is thus that the birthday of our Saviour Jesus Christ is kept in England! And this example I select from a multitude, because this manner of amusement is the contrary of merry. The word "merry," so the American philologer Whitney informs us, has no cognate word in the Teutonic languages; from the conquered Celts, in whose language it meant "a child's game," the Anglo-Saxons took it to express delight at the beauty of a landscape, particularly of woods and meadows; Shakespeare still calls the humming of the bees "merry"; from this meaning it assumed the signification of joy in music, particularly in singing, and this third stage then grew to mean "innocent gaiety" in general.

In this so peculiarly descriptive word the former English people were adequately described. And I do not think that any competent Englishman will contradict me when I say, "We were merry, we are no longer so."

With the complete decay of country life, and the just as complete victory of the god of commerce and industry, mammon, all true, harmless, simple, heart-easing merriment has departed from England. And this again recalls an old proverb, "'Tis good to be merry and wise," and the merry man is certainly the wise one, and he who is not merry is certainly not wise.

I believe I can maintain with certainty that the catastrophe of the complete loss of English merriment, of English wisdom, of English honesty (for this, too, was proverbial in former times), is due to the circumstance that the change to war, trade, and piracy came upon a people split into two peculiar classes. All civilisation, religion, education, army, art, legislation, customs, presupposes unity, if it is to penetrate the whole nation in such a manner that even the simplest man receives something from it. What is meant by this is well known in Germany, and I need dwell no longer on it. In England it is unknown. As soon as the honest Anglo-Saxon peasant had been converted into a pirate, then we had the "blond beast," as he is described by the German philologer, Nietzsche, in his mad dreams; and as soon as the "refined" noble had lost intellectual interests and become greedy for gold there arose the heartless slave-trader, who only differed from the Spanish brutal tyrant by his hypocrisy. There is nothing more brutal in the world than a brutal Englishman. He has no other resource than his brutality. Generally speaking, he is not a bad man; he is frank, energetic, full of animal spirits, but he is as ignorant as a Kaffir; passes through no school of discipline and respect; knows no other ideal than to "fight his way through." This brutality has gradually permeated from the bottom to the top—as is always the case—nearly the whole nation. Only fifty years ago it was regarded as derogatory for a member of the nobility to take part in industry, commerce, or finance. To-day, the head of the greatest family of Scotland, the brother-in-law of the king, is a banker! Sons of earls and dukes disappear from society; if you ask what has become of them, you are told, "Oh, he is making his heap." Where and in what manner nobody asks. Suddenly, he returns as a rich man, and all is well.

In the meanwhile another kind of brutality has developed in the upper caste, which is still more serious in regard to politics. Although external customs and refined manners have remained the same, the moral compass seems to have grown unreliable. The temptation of great power founded on immense wealth seems to have been too great. Among the nobility and those connected with it, they seem no longer to be able to distinguish between right and wrong. The same man who in private life would never sway a hair's breadth from the path of the strictest integrity, commits, in the supposed interest of his country, any crime. The prophets among us—Burke, Carlyle, Ruskin—have, for the last hundred years, been deploring the decay of veracity, which was formerly so holy in England. For this, too, I should like to give an example. The reader will see into what ways, or, rather, what errors, England has fallen.

The name of Warren Hastings will be known to nearly all. As a mere youth he entered the service of the East India Company. He rose to Governor-General. Doubtlessly, England owes her dominion over India, in the first place, to this man, who with Machiavellian cunning found the means of setting the different countries, races, religions, and dynasties of India against each other, and inciting them all against the competition of the French. Together with eminent intellectual properties and a will of iron, Warren Hastings is particularly distinguished by a complete lack of scruple in political matters. He was connected with tyrants like Tipu Sahib, with criminals who, from the lowest castes, forced their way to the throne, and then, like wild beasts, ruled over the patient Hindoo, with sorceresses on the throne, who kept their own sons in dungeons that they might continue to wallow in the blood of the people, with the worst scum of Asiatic monsters, into whose power unfortunate India had fallen. Certainly mild measures were of no avail here, and if the Company, or rather the English government which stood behind it, had intervened with strong, armed hand, they would have done a noble task. There was no question of this. The government never thought of assisting with money or soldiers, and the Company did not wish to increase its expenditure, but to raise its revenue. And so Warren Hastings now joined issue with one Indian prince and now with another, raised no questions of right or wrong, even protected the greatest villain of a usurper as long as he served the interests of the Company, and, as he thought, those of England best. Above all things money was necessary. How was he otherwise to procure and equip an army? India must pay for her own subjection. And so Hastings selected among the rival princes those who promised the largest sums of money. These he supported with all the means over which a European could dispose. In this manner he nearly doubled the revenue of the East India Company. How was it possible? How could these princes pay such sums and supply so many soldiers? By the means of such atrocities the like of which the world has never heard of until the noble Belgians occupied the Congo—atrocities which left an eternal stain upon the name of humanity, for no animal could imagine them, and no devil would dare to practise them on innocent beings.

Then, in 1786, the great Burke arose—immortal by this deed alone—and by the enthusiasm of his words prevailed upon Parliament to proceed against the man who was thus disgracing England's good name. When the case was brought before the House of Lords, the highest court of appeal, Burke spoke six days in succession, founding the accusation in every detail and terminating with the words: "I accuse Warren Hastings in the name of the eternal laws of all justice, I accuse him in the name of human nature which he has covered with disgrace."

The case dragged on for ten years, that is to say, it was protracted by all legal means and tricks. One can imagine how the distance of India, at that time, rendered difficult the procuring of testimony and retarded the proceedings, and to what an extent Hastings and the Company profited from this. It was always repeated: he had raised the revenue from £3,000,000 to £5,000,000, what more do you want? Even at the present day these figures are to be found in nearly all English books on the subject; Hastings is considered justified. Besides, he had invented the opium trade. Should such a genius be punished? Pitt, as

Prime Minister, conversant with the documents of the accusation, said, "There is only one means of escape; he must plead urgency of state matters." In short, Hastings was acquitted. Burke, in the last of his great speeches in the court, his attempt to obtain victory for the good cause—he had repeatedly fainted from exhaustion while delivering it—pronounced the ever-memorable words: "My lords, if you close your eyes to these atrocities you make of us Englishmen a nation of concealers, a nation of hypocrites, a nation of liars, a nation of cheats; the character of England, that character which more than our arms, more than our trade, has made a great nation of us, England's character will be destroyed, lost for ever. Truly, we also know the power of money, and we feel it, but against it we appeal to your lordships, that you should procure justice, that you may save our morals and our virtues, that you may protect our national character and our liberty."

The day on which Warren Hastings was acquitted—April 23rd, 1795—is one of those days of which I spoke at the commencement of this essay, when history and character clash, and we suddenly gain an insight into the interior. New England, which of course had long been in the process of evolution from the old, now stood as an accomplished fact. Hastings had not amassed personal wealth, he had not in his private capacity cheated other individuals; he had, perhaps, in his life not harmed a fly; yet in the interest of his country—that is to say, of its power and wealth—he had feared no lie, no perjury, had betrayed those who confided in him, had not protected the innocent, and placed criminals on the throne. He had suffered that others committed cruelties of the most revolting nature by simply turning his back and refusing to take notice of them; had dismissed English officials, who reported them with horror. We see the modern English statesman is an accomplished fact at the same time as modern England.

Exactly such a man is Sir Edward Grey; for years gone by he has presided at peace conferences, so that the intended war should, by no means, fail to be brought about. For years he has sought "rapprochement" to Germany, so that the honest German statesmen and diplomatists should not perceive the firm intention of the war of annihilation. In the last moment the German Emperor nearly warded off the danger of the war. Grey, the canting apostle of peace, finds means to shuffle the cards in such a manner that it is impossible. England had always shuddered at the thought of regicide; now that the unheard-of crime takes place, that state officials and officers prepare it, and that the heir to a throne causes the heir to the neighbouring throne to be murdered, now not a word of horror, but Grey discovers England's mission to protect the "little states." The English government causes

Antwerp, in "neutral Belgium," to be converted into the strongest fortress in the world; the English government had already sent ammunition to Maubeuge in 1913. Grey had the military convention between France and Belgium in his pocket; all details of landing, transport, etc., are drawn up, black on white, and yet he finds means to make it appear that it is Germany which—from pure necessity, we know now that it would otherwise have been lost—"breaks the neutrality." For the first time in the history of the world the whole English fleet was mobilised—but only for a harmless *revue* by the king. Just at the time of the assassination of Francis Ferdinand a friendly visit to Kiel is arranged, for all attempts to spy out this harbour had failed.

That is the political England of to-day, as Burke had prophesied—concealers, hypocrites, liars, cheats. Ruskin gives us bitter comfort: "Let us take no heed of this England, in a hundred years it will belong to the dead nations." Nor do I believe in the monstrous strength of England, of which we hear so much; real strength can only stand on a firm moral foundation. The individual Englishman is brave and honest; the English state is rotten to the core. It need but be firmly tackled.

Germany is so entirely different that for years she did not understand England, the political England of to-day, and always allowed herself to be deceived anew. I nearly fear that this will happen again in the future. That might be fateful. Therefore, I, an Englishman, must have the courage to bear testimony to the truth. A strong, wise, victorious Germany alone can save us all.

VI.

GERMANY.

VI.

GERMANY.

VERY frequently one hears of late the question, "Why do all nations hate Germany and the Germans?" This question, coming from the mouth of a real German can, in such times, have a touching effect.

If there is in the world a peaceful, well-behaved, pious people it is the Germans. The good education which each, without exception, receives; the spirit of discipline which prevails throughout public life; their naturally reflexive disposition, all contribute to curb the more brutal elements and to assure the prevalence of the temperate. And these qualities are not of recent date; they are only more pronounced at present than formerly, because Germany has been incessantly educating herself. Towards the end of his career Napoleon stated that in all his campaigns in Germany he did not lose a single soldier by assassination; of other countries he could not maintain the same.

And one must bear in mind what vengeful hatred the Germans must have borne against the French, who had repeatedly converted the most beautiful parts of their country into deserts—not soldiers against soldiers, but a furious horde of inhuman savages, hurled against a harmless population. And yet no revenge, no lust for blood, not a single case. Nowhere a single German, who, unobserved, far from restraining discipline, falls upon a sleeping or a straying Frenchman; among millions of inhabitants not one. And this testimony comes from the cold-hearted enemy of Germany! On the other hand, let us cast a glance at the "Franctireurs" of 1870-71, the treacherous murderers, who deprived hundreds or, perhaps, even thousands of brave German soldiers of their lives. Cast a glance at the wounded Zouaves and Turcos, who bit off the fingers of the Red Cross men; think of the English campaigns against the Matabeles and other peaceful Zulu tribes in the nineties, in which the terrible dum-dum bullets were used to hasten the end of all resistance. Think of the revolting atrocities which the Belgians practised for years in the Congo on a harmless, unarmed people, solely for money, to force the people by the fear of death to hard work. Read the officially accredited report signed by priests on the conduct of the Belgian civil population of both sex in the present war, who, worse than wild beasts, gouged out the eyes of the poor German wounded, maimed them in other ways, and then suffocated them by pouring sawdust into their mouths and noses. It is unnecessary to speak of Russian atrocities, as this nation makes no claim to civilisation.

And still these nations enjoy the sympathies of the world and are extolled as civilising powers, whereas the German is called barbarian, incendiary, murderer, so that the whole population flee at the approach of a German soldier, the only one of reliable discipline, who has never harmed a hair on the head of an innocent man. I should, indeed, like to know what other army is accompanied by professional art critics, whose duty it is immediately on the occupation of a town to take charge of the treasures of art found there. At the first entry of the Germans into Rheims this year, I hear by private letter, the soldiers were conducted through the cathedral by professional connoisseurs and crowded round, as many as could obtain leave, in pious contemplation. And yet everyone believes the slander that the German armies intentionally destroy treasures of art. What we experienced forty-four years ago is repeated in the present universal war. Every Frenchman, every Belgian, every Englishman and

Russian who really comes into contact with German soldiers is astonished not only at their iron discipline, but also what honest, absolutely decent, good-hearted men they are. The belief in the monstrosity of the Germans is so deeply rooted that personal experiences are regarded as exceptions and not counted in the general account. This was the case in 1870. I can speak from wide experience. For, at that time, I possessed in France, where I had spent the first years of my life, many and some very intimate relations. At the end of 1871 I was again in France. Everywhere the same story. Not a single Frenchman have I met who stated that he had suffered cruelty himself or even excessive harshness, or seen it practised on others. But the inhabitants of my beloved Versailles assured: "The king was here and the 'great Head-quarters,' so the men were careful; but if you knew how the barbarians behaved in Normandy!" Now just in Normandy I had old relations to peasant families. I made enquiries. "No," I was told, "we were fortunate. Manteufel's army was operating here, excellent men, irreproachable discipline, they dare not have pinched an egg; but in Alsace—there it must have been terrible." The eastern country was unknown to me, but in that winter I made the acquaintance of a French Alsatian pastor, violent German hater, but a truthful man, and when I put the old question to him he drew a sketch-book from his drawer and showed me a gigantic German infantryman engaged in peeling potatoes in the kitchen of his manse, a Uhlan sitting on a stone bench before the door feeding with tender clumsiness a baby, and other similar idyllic scenes. "Quelle bonne pâte d'hommes," he cried, nearly enthusiastically, "and what good-natured fellows!" But then followed the usual: "But we were lucky, they were Pomeranians who stayed longest in our town; but if you knew how the South Germans in the Orléannais have behaved."

Even such evident nonsense as that the Germans carried away all clocks is not to be eradicated; for years I have been on the look-out for a Frenchman who lost a clock, but my search has always been in vain. And still the belief is so firm that in the present war—as the papers report—in some places the inhabitants place their clocks outside their doors as a kind of reconciliatory sacrifice. I can only say it shows how true it is that human fancy leads human reason by the nose. It is true any of us who has travelled has met German men and women who did not distinguish themselves by grace and modesty, and caused a very disadvantageous idea of what is German; but those of us who have experienced Frenchmen and Italians abroad can tell of worse things still. Like Treitschke, I have often been annoyed at Englishmen. But these are not things to arouse national hatred. No, this hatred has general, wide-spreading roots and, as it has once sprung into existence, it causes every lie about Germany and the Germans to find ready credence, however incredible or unprovable it may be. For many people it is a pleasure to speak evil of the Germans, and by slander to deprive them of respect.

We have just now experienced again that men who, like the French musician Jaques-Dalcroze, after long wandering over the earth, in Germany alone found appreciation for their new ideals of art, unselfish assistance and a home, are not ashamed of accusing Germany of deliberately destroying towns and intentionally annihilating treasures of art. Not only a revolting, but so absolutely stupid slander, that it is hard to understand how an intelligent man who has spent but one day in Germany can render himself so ridiculous. As love gives insight, so does hate make blind. And from this case we see that even benevolence and unselfish assistance are not sufficient to gain love for Germany; German generosity does but produce ingratitude and treachery.

The fact of the hatred cannot be denied; it extends from the more or less concealed dislike of refined minds to the bloodthirsty rage of the brutal, to the treachery of the cowardly subscribers of the Geneva protest.

I, personally, adhering to the tactics of immortal Moltke, have the habit of answering the above question, Why is Germany so hated? by advancing to the attack with the question: Why is Germany so loved? Not that I consider the matter settled in this manner; but this counter-question gives rise to reflection and raises the dispute into a higher sphere which, at least with all questions concerning Germany, is an advantage. Carlyle alone, and even if he were the only one of modern times, would be sufficient to give us something to think of for a long time. For Carlyle, thanks to lifelong studies, was intimately acquainted with the German mind, and it is always an advantage to know what you are about to criticise. Carlyle had the great advantage that he not only knew literary Germany from the most ancient times up to Goethe, but he had also studied the development of the nation, as it stands before us to-day, so that for him, with his prophetic talent, the past, the present, and the future lay clear before his eyes. No one has written more beautifully on Luther than Carlyle. He knew him thoroughly, and it is to be regretted that his strength did not last for the intended biography.

It is not the theologian that entrances him, it is the man of God, the German man. From Luther's room in the Wartburg he writes: "One feels that of all places upon which the sun shines down, this for us living ones is the most holy. To me at least, in my poor thoughts, it would seem as if the direct presence of God sanctified these rooms, as if eternal memories and holy influences, warning precepts were hovering around whispering to the hearts of men painful, powerful and brave words." And then Carlyle relates how his companion—I believe it was Emerson—when he believed himself unobserved, quickly bent down and impressed an ardent kiss on the old oak table. These two foreigners knew Germany and therefore loved it. "Noble, patient, deep-minded, pious, able Germany," as Carlyle called it in 1870. For Luther is not a great man who happened to be born in Germany; he and his native land rather form the front and the reverse of a coin, which on the one side shows, as if seen in a dream, the symbol of unutterable forces, desires, doubts, and delights of a millionfold endeavours, and on the other perishable features of a man in whose life that which all desired has assumed eternal form. Luther and Germany are so inseparable, so closely interwoven as—at the other end of the possible scale of human talents—this is the case between Goethe and Germany. To bring forth great men of this description a people must possess great qualities. Tieck wrote the true words: "As soon as Goethe opened his eyes and opened those of others, Germany stood there in her direct existence." She had but slumbered.

Germany, and perhaps this is a symbol of her productive force, periodically relaxes into unconsciousness of herself and must be awakened by a message from above; never did the trumpet-sound which calls to the fulfilment of eternal duties ring more powerfully than through Luther, a direct product of the native earth, and immediately raised a loud echo throughout the whole German people, from prince to peasant. Each recognised the voice of his own conscience, as he had heard it between his dreams. Why has the Reformation never gained a firm foothold in Bohemia, in Poland, in France, in England? Because everywhere it was a matter of sects. Whereas in Luther the longing of a whole people for truth is expressed, and it, therefore, had the same effect on those who remained faithful to Rome as on those who broke away. With him it is not a question of religion in the sense of any Church, but of religion which includes the whole sphere of life and teaches to regard one's native country as the most holy of God's gifts. Therefore, one can and must say that Germany who stands so powerfully to-day is Luther's Germany. She speaks his language, thinks his thoughts, and does the deeds that he desired. Dogmatic questions lie outside the pale of German thoughts. He who knows Luther well therefore knows Germany well; that was the case with Carlyle. And now a curious coincidence happened. Carlyle, at the age of twenty-one, was so conversant with the German character that he could write a life of Schiller, felt, when he had matured into a man, as a task desired by God (he tells us so himself) the necessity of giving up twenty years of his life to the study of Frederick the Great. Through this, his insight became perfect, for now he had become intimately acquainted with the driving force of the political renaissance of Germany and could estimate its power.

Carlyle was not a hero-worshipper in the restricted sense of the word. He had no veneration for the meteoric hero, who passes, no one knows from where, bound for some indefinite port, lacking all substance, and when he once, for the sake of a system, wished to write on Napoleon, he broke off after three pages with the words, "Poor man." No, the true hero grows out of the community as a condensed expression of all the forces divided in individuals, thus to carry away the community to attainments for which it is adapted, but to the accomplishment of which it would never have proceeded without this incomparable hero. Richard Wagner offers the best example of our times; his art would never have been able to contend victoriously against a sea of hate and slander had it not corresponded to the particular longings and hopes of the German soul, realising what thousands had seen in dark dreams and a few had sought, groping their way, but what only one divine genius was capable of giving. In what does the real sanctity of human greatness consist? To be the man whom all need, for he alone needs all men and sets the whole in motion. No word in Carlyle's great work deserves more attention than his praise of Prussia in the first chapter of the twenty-first book:

"Brave Prussia; but the real soul of its merit was that of having merited such a king to command it. An accidental merit, thinks the reader?

"No, reader, you may believe me, it is by no means altogether such. Nay, I rather think, could we look into the Account Book of the Recording Angel for a course of centuries, no part of it is such! There are nations in which a Friedrich is or can be possible; and again there are nations in which he is and can not be. Nations who have lost this quality, or who have never had it, what Friedrich can they ever hope to be possible among them?"

This remark is of the greatest importance, for besides the obscene abusers of Germany there are a host of false friends of the school of Lord Haldane, who assert that they love Germany, ideal Germany, the Germany of poetry, philosophy, and music; Germany dedicated to pure science. They detest only militarism and its stronghold Prussia, and would like to root it out, whereas here we hear the man who really knows the intellectual and political history of Germany and recognises its organic unity, and he says with no uncertain voice:—

"This assertion is either folly or insincere hypocrisy; for without Prussia there would be no Germany to-day, and without that great school of veneration of true human dignity which is slightingly styled 'militarism' there would be no Prussia. A great people need political greatness, and a noble, patient, deep-minded, honest people deserve to be their own masters, deserve to possess that influence which belongs to them and to use it in the interest of humanity."

The foreigner who pretends to love Germany without Prussia is—excuse the harsh expression, but there are times when things must be called by their proper names—either a blockhead or a rogue. Carlyle alone weighs up a thousand muddle-headed Haldanes, to say nothing of all the leader-writers in Europe. How stupid envy and hate make people! Three great nations have for years been arming and have formed a criminal conspiracy to attack Germany—the peaceful, industrious country that threatened no one—and to destroy it. Thanks to Providence, so many secret documents have been brought to the light of day, that no man of calm judgment can have the slightest doubt that the so-called "restrictive policy" simply meant a diabolical attack, a raid of brigands, prearranged in all its details, upon a troublesome competitor; and because Germany—the wise, the honest, the brave—sets up an iron defence, fights with gigantic forces, therefore it is defiled as the stronghold of militarism and held up to execration. It is as if burglars were to complain because the police had spoilt their well-conceived plan, and to show moral indignation on this account. It would seem at times as if one had to do with silly boys incapable of stringing three ideas together. How can one talk of "militarism" in regard to an army in which every second officer is either a professor, a merchant, or a lawyer? In Russia "militarism" has ruled for years, and leads to crime after crime to delay the dawn of the day of judgment which will sweep away all who have governed so dishonourably. In France a government of adventurers rules the all too patient and too weak people; adventurers who, to hide their shady financial transactions, and keep their manipulations from becoming evident in the general confusion, stimulate the cry of revenge. Truly the most contemptible kind of "militarism." And a government like the English, which of long date has been planning a raid upon a closely related, peaceful neighbour, may rightly be described as "militaristic," for by means of battleships and force of arms it desires to deprive the other of the fruits of his industry and to appropriate them. But where all men for the defence of their country, of their livelihood, of their individuality take to the field, led by all their princes, that is not "militarism," but a nation in arms. There they lie in the German trenches beside each other—prince, banker, engineer, schoolmaster, artisan, tradesman, workman, and peasant—the whole German nation of men; the professional soldier disappears in their masses. But that the professional soldier is there, that he has been there throughout the long years of peace, may God requite him for it in all eternity! Without him Germany would now hopelessly succumb to the criminal Coalition. And he is the creation of Frederick the Great and his successors; the creation of Stein, Scharnhorst, Gneisenau, and many others; in short, the creation of Prussia. The South

German has the same staying powers and fights as well as the North German. We have seen that in 1870 and 1914; but the genius of organisation, the strained alertness, the never-relaxing readiness, the marvellous faculty of being always prepared to spring, that is Prussia's merit. Carlyle has a beautiful expression for it: "Like the stars, always steady at his work." That is the motto I would have inscribed in golden letters over the entrance of the office of the General Staff in Berlin in honour of these magnificent men: "The constancy of stars." Therefore, false, seeming friends, cease your prattle about militarism, or uncover your heads and bow "in humility before human dignity." If the army is the backbone of Germany to-day, it is because it has deserved to be the backbone. The German army (in which I, of course, include the navy) is the most important institution of moral education in the world. Discipline can be enforced by a Dschengis Khan, but through it he only produces wild beasts. But the German army—thanks to the Hohenzollern and the Prussian spirit—trains to obedience and, at the same time, to self-respect, to patience, to action, to exactitude and resourcefulness. The present war proves this a thousandfold. We may go still further, for the spirit of the German army has already penetrated the whole life of the nation, and is the key to German success in all quarters. By teaching, on the one hand, the exact and conscientious collaboration of the mass for a definite purpose, each one subordinating himself to the whole as an obedient, modest, zealous collaborator, seeking reward and satisfaction in the attainments of the whole, and, on the other hand, it attains the development of the incomparable exactitude for which the 42 cm. mortars have become known throughout the world, but which to the same extent is working in a thousand places—in chemical laboratories, in engineering works, in manufactories of all descriptions, in scientific enterprises, and, in time, will be evident everywhere. If, in addition, the average degree of education be taken into consideration, which has been enormously raised by the collaboration of school and army in Germany, it is clear how much of the excellent attainments of Germany, in many spheres which are still capable of enormous development, may rightly be attributed to the spirit of the army. The characteristic and distinctive feature is that this German military spirit, unlike the English naval spirit, which only rouses the instinct of piracy, has contributed to the attainments of peace. Cooperation and precision are the newest discoveries of the human mind, which intensify its attainments a hundredfold. While natural science was revealing itself in the sphere of theory, it invented, in its dire necessity, in the sphere of practical life, the Hohenzollern monarchy. There have been many armies in the world, but that an army should have developed a soul of its own, a "spiritus rector," and that this should be "perfection," that was a new invention of nature.

"The love of perfection in work done" is what Carlyle calls the main feature of Frederick William I.'s character and of his son's. So different in all other things, in this they resembled each other. In these two things—co-operation and precision—in the gradual solution of the many problems, which the realisation of such ideals imposes upon the mind of man, lies the spirit of the Prussian army, which to-day has become the spirit of the whole united German army. But this spirit is the spirit of the whole of the enterprising German nation. In it and by it Germany marches at the head of all the nations in the world.

Only so much to-day about the foolish reproach of "militarism." One sees how good it is to get to the bottom of things. Lord Haldane, the learned Minister of State, Ph.D. of Göttingen, LL.D. of Edinburgh, etc., could by a little reflection have saved himself the trouble of writing incoherent nonsense. The same refers to the many others who have raised the same point. But enough of these slanderers of German honour; let us sweep them all into a common grave and return to our question: "Why is Germany so loved?"

The love of Germany, for which Carlyle finds such glowing words, is by no means new. It can be traced back centuries. How enthusiastically the Germans have always loved their native land I do not need to point out to Germans. It might, however, be mentioned in this connection, for how should a country be loved so tenderly by so many high and powerful minds if it were barbaric and detestable? I will but recall one stanza of Walter von der Vogelweide:

"I've roved afar through many lands,
And have enjoyed the best,
But may some evil me befall
If there my heart found rest;

Though foreign customs pleased me well,
Why should I the truth not tell ?
German life excels them all."

In this two things are particularly worthy of note. The entire lack of animosity against foreign things, of which the minstrel "enjoyed the best," and the emphasis laid on the fact that the Germans are distinguished by good education, decent morals and customs. These lines were written about 1200; even at that period the people—whom Maeterlinck, Bourget, Rolland, Shaw, etc., would like to decry as barbarians—were superior to all others in moral "education." Exactly the quality which to-day distinguishes the German people as a whole, with a few exceptions which will, it is to be hoped, now be exterminated, from the chaotic licence of their tango-dancing neighbours. But not only Germans judge Germany so favourably. I can call a foreign witness of such great import that all slanders fade before him. No less a man than Michel de Montaigne shall bear testimony to the truth. Among the present detractors of Germany, none dare deny that Montaigne is one of the most intellectual and independent men who ever lived in Europe; for us it is also of importance that he belonged to the nobility, had spent a long time at the French court, and was a far-travelled man, knowing the world and men as hardly any other did, and seeing to the bottom of things.

In the year 1581 he travelled in Germany for pleasure, and was so pleased that he said: "I left it with real grief, although my way lay towards Italy." He sums up his impressions in the following words: "Tout y est plein de commodité et de courtoisie, et surtout de justice et de sûreté." Four things, then, according to the criticism of the Frenchman, distinguish Germany of the sixteenth century: comfort, politeness, justice, and safety. In the itinerary from which I take this extract, Montaigne repeatedly refers to the excellent installation and management of the German inns, particularly in comparison with the terrible conditions in France. He also quotes many examples of politeness which he, at times, even experienced as inconvenient; so, for instance, the custom, which still strikes us Western Europeans and which, as we here see, existed at that time, of letting persons whom one wished to honour walk at one's right hand. Thus, so it was explained to the Chevalier, allowing the stranger, at any moment, to draw his sword, for which, however, especially in Germany, there was no occasion. Externally, then, in regard to customs, decency, and politeness, Germany stood as high as France, if not higher; and, internally, no less so. For right and justice together with the security of person and property form the foundations of every higher civilisation and culture. If, therefore, Germany distinguished itself in these, it means that it was, at that time, the most civilised country in Europe. Hardly arrived in Bozen and

Trient, Montaigne longs once more for the "charm of the German towns," and in Rome he soon had occasion to form a different idea of personal security, for, as he relates, the Pope and the cardinals, in spite of the official tasters, dare not drink the wine at communion otherwise than by means of specially constructed golden tubes so as to avoid, as far as possible, the constant danger of being poisoned!

Then the terrible Thirty Years' War came. It was over with the "charm of German towns." Whose fault was this catastrophe? To speak of a war of creeds does not fathom the matter; many other things are involved; if a quantity of subsidiary matters are set aside, the main issue is a war between the really German element and the not really German element; only then one sees that the thirty years with the artificial peace are insufficient, but that the war lasted with interruptions for two and a half centuries, only being brought to a conclusion in 1866, when the vital centre was once more placed in old real German country from whence it had started, that is to say, in the North.

If we review in thought the whole of this time, commencing soon after the time of Montaigne's pleasant journey, at a time when the confessions dwelt peacefully side by side and mixed marriages were of daily occurrence in Augsburg, up to the moment when Bismarck set his hand to the task, we shall be surprised at the Divine guidance, thanks to which there proceeded from the seemingly chaotic important consequences working one upon each other, and step by step the fragments of dissolution were collected, and once more united, again increased in essence and strength. They formed new organisations, derived advantages from peace and war, from victory and defeat, for external and internal development until, at last, the great, magnificent nation was attained, admirable in diversity, incomparable in material and mental treasures, exceeding all others in energy. Thus we succeed in looking upon the disastrous Thirty Years' War, which nearly caused the destruction of Germany, as an episode in a process of fermentation, of convalescence, of purification; as a necessary transformation in order to adapt itself to a new time which demanded new forms, a process which ultimately proved to be to Germany's advantage, because during this time of trial in the hidden depths of her essential being she remained true to herself and, therefore, pure.

I know of nothing more touching and more sublime in the history of mankind than the development of the purely ideal art of music to its highest perfection by the Thuringian family Bach, in the midst of all the sins and atrocities of this period. Richard Wagner, who was the first to call attention to this in his Essay, "What is German?" says of Johann Sebastian: "Bach teaches us to see what the German spirit really is, where it was taking refuge and indefatigably recreating itself, at a time when it seemed to have disappeared from the world. No other people possesses anything similar, not only nothing like Bach, but nothing like this great process of purification of two and a half centuries' duration; nothing similar to this tranquil formation and re-formation of the soul in hidden depths. And the consequence is that Germany to-day stands among all the old nations as the only youthful one; she has been born again, she alone. Her classical poetry and prose, her most sublime music, her dramatic perfection, all were attained on the threshold of the nineteenth century, or in the nineteenth century; they belong to the living generation as a power which idealises the rough trivialities of daily life. Whereas the English and French productions of the same standing lie centuries back, testimonies of a world that has passed away. At the same time, and it is at least as remarkable, Germany alone has preserved from times gone by, besides mental treasures of all kinds, living political organisations which everywhere else have disappeared in favour of empty, abstract uniformity. Thus Germany issues from her long and hard trial rich in new things and rich in old, unique.

Doubtlessly the incapacity of people of the present day to understand and love Germany is connected with the process of which we have just treated. Of Old Germany, which Montaigne loved so well, they know nothing, for New Germany they are themselves too old, or, let us use the favourite term for once in its right application—too barbaric—to be able to comprehend it. For the querulous old men who hobble about on the worn-out crutches of abstract liberty and equality do not understand that liberty can only be gained by the sacrifice of personal licence, and equality found only in the general subordination of all to a common goal, not by each soldier being a Field-Marshal, as is the case in Haiti. They have stuck fast in the ideas of the seventeenth and eighteenth centuries, of a time when Germany did not know herself, when Germany as a moral unity had disappeared from sight and formed only a chaos. That is the Germany they wish for, that they would like to see rise up again. They did not know if they should consider the Emperor "of German nationality," but who was not of German nationality, as the centre of the country. But one thing they did know, that the King of Prussia who waged war against the imperial power could certainly not be a German. And so, in the end, between "Autrichien" and "Prussien," the idea "Allemand" had entirely disappeared from the world; Germany was hardly spoken of.

Doubtlessly the chief crime of the present Empire in the eyes of its adversaries, and the chief cause of the hatred which saddens so many an honest German soul, is founded on nothing else but the existence of Germany. It was so fearfully convenient for England

and France not to have to reckon with Germany as a stable, lasting factor. Napoleon treated it as a cook does his jelly, which he can divide and put together as he likes, and now, all of a sudden, it was no longer jelly, but a fact as hard as steel, that could not be cleared out of the way. Instead of jelly, General Staff, that was bitter. The easy-going Germany that fought England's battles and then served as a footstool for England at the Congress of Vienna had passed away. An extremely inconvenient Germany placed the strongest army in the world in the field and set about building a corresponding fleet. In accordance with the old saying, "Tout comprendre c'est tout pardonner," I cannot help feeling some compassion for the noble lord, whom we have just borne to his grave, and who pretended to love Germany without her "militarism." And no one knew—nor do they know today—how the transformation took place. It smacks of witchcraft. All English historians firmly maintain (so Carlyle relates) that Frederick the Great—one of the most noble men in the history of the world—was a "robber" and a "villain." From these two assertions they proceed to further comprehension. That is the tone henceforth in which all are treated who in any way have contributed to the transformation of "jelly" to General Staff. Bismarck, whose greatness is, not to the least extent, founded on his gigantic frankness, is never mentioned in the *Times* without the epithet "forger," or the terrifying qualification "man of blood and iron," thus caricaturing Bismarck's beautiful saying and committing a double perfidy.

In all this a grudging disposition, envy, jealousy, and powerless rage are betrayed. It would, however, be a mistake to seek any historic foundation for this hate. Not once in the course of the history of the world has Germany done England any harm. No, it is not the past, but the present which is cast up to Germany as a crime. The fact that from the state of annihilation into which she seemed to have sunk—seemed on superficial observation, for politicians pay no attention to art, philosophy, and science—now suddenly she has become something powerful: powerful in her capacity to deal heavy blows, powerful in creation, in invention, in diligence, in intelligence, in enterprise, in success, and—most unheard of—in financial means. This Germany in truth—not only the pretended "militarism," especially the English hate and "to hate" means in its original sense "to hunt to death."

Perhaps the majority have no conception how far the idea of having to reckon with a Germany of political importance had disappeared from the eyes of Western Europe. For them Germany was a harmless country to which to resort, in the age when one is troubled by gout and liver ailments, to drink the waters. I remember, as if it were yesterday, the descriptions that were given me of Germany when I was a child. Before every house there was a dunghill, upon the dunghill sat half-starved, half-naked boys and read Schiller. As late as the year 1889 I purchased on the Eiffel Tower a French guide-book in which could be read that Cologne was noted for its cathedral and on account of "les sources odoriférantes qui y coulent," so certain were they that Germans were incapable of producing anything that they even caused our dear "Eau de Cologne" to spring as a well out of the ground. But, joking apart, consult the scholars, for instance, the French "encyclopédistes" and their contemporaries, you will soon discover how pale their conception of Germany was. In the great "Encyclopédie" the word "Allemagne" occupies hardly half a column, and the half of this half-column is dedicated to a commercial treaty with Turkey. In Diderot, Bayle, Rousseau, the word hardly occurs. Old lynx-eyed Voltaire seems occasionally to catch a glimpse of future trouble.

After a description of the second systematical devastation of the Palatinate in 1689, he warns the French, if once the Germans should come to their senses, they would be capable of placing a much larger army in the field than the French, at the same time one of much better discipline and greater powers of resistance.

He often mocks at the English method to fight with bribes and subsidies instead of soldiers, and if forced to use them, to resort to foreign auxiliaries. Then in a prophetic moment he sees what a mighty power might arise in Germany, "si jamais ce vaste pays pouvait être réuni sous un seul chef," should ever the day come when the whole country would obey one single War Lord. On the other hand, it would not appear to me that Voltaire had any conception of what distinguished Germany as a people, as a national soul, as it had appealed to the Chevalier de Montaigne in so pleasing a manner after his short sojourn. He fails to understand how from the ruined chaos, which, at that time, was called Germany, a nation was ever to be made. Once in a letter to Frederick the Great, which for the moment I cannot find and, therefore, cannot quote textually, he expresses his astonishment at the difference between North and South; how in Prussia intelligence and character are everywhere displayed, whereas the South of Germany seemed to stick in a quagmire of stupid superstition, hopelessly abandoned to suffocation. Who would have predicted that the North would succeed in arousing the South? That in the twentieth century we should have the sublime spectacle of a united Germany fighting shoulder to shoulder from the North Sea to the Adriatic, from the Vosges to the Carpathians!

If foreigners do not love Germany, it is because they do not know it; they do not get to know it, because old-fashioned ideas block the way to knowledge. It should, however, be observed here that Germany, for a long time, had forgotten herself, and only by degrees has she again arrived at a proper estimation of her own value. Indeed, I venture to maintain still more. If I forget the present moment, which shows the whole population exalted and transfigured, if I look back upon the ordinary everyday life of Germany, I see many Germans who neither know nor love Germany—modern Germany—as she deserves to be known and loved. I do not wish to hint that they are not good patriots, far from me, but they grumble and grouse at this and that, are narrow-minded and short-sighted, and from their point of view are as little satisfied with modern Germany as the foreigners are from theirs. The policy of Germany since 1870, and particularly since the shaping of the "New Course," cannot be overlooked from the village steeple. In this sour mood—it is not pronounced enough to be called bitter—lies a longing for past times and conditions, a weakly sentimentalism which is not a true product of German life and feeling. A poison such as Heine's poetry is not imbibed with impunity, and generations of young men and women have suffered from its effects and suffer still. And this is the poison which those foreigners imbibe who spend a few months or years in Germany for their education, and who certainly might have acquired something better. It is absolutely untrue that the real poets and thinkers of Germany stand on one side and the soldiers and practical men upon the other as two separate opposing representatives of Germanism.

With flying colours the German poet marches at the head of the nation:

> " 'Twere vain and useless to attempt
> To stop th' eternal wheel of time
> With wings the hours bear it on,
> The new things come, the old are gone."

And as far as the soldiers are concerned, I heard the other day from a publisher that in the Western frontier towns all copies of Goethe's "Faust" had been sold out. No book has been taken to the front in such quantities. And the German poets deserve this honourable love of the soldiers. Apart from men like Kleist, Theodor Körner, Ernst Moritz, Arndt, all the greatest German poets distinguish themselves by the importance they attach to national development, and their longing to see it strong and powerful, in a manner which I have been unable to discover in any other literature. That their sentiments do not apply to the present moment as those of the poets of the war of liberation, adds more weight to the assertion. After Waterloo, Beethoven rejoices that the German nation "has once more regained its strength," and it is certainly worthy of remark when such a man confesses: "Strength is the moral power of those who distinguish themselves before others, it is also mine." And Schiller says: "The strong alone can overcome the fates."

Being an historian as well as a poet, he wrote the well-known verse which might have been composed for the present day:

> "Greedy as the arms of octopus
> Britain sends her ships afar
> And the realm of Neptunus
> Closes with a mighty bar."

Schiller knows, as you see, that England is the selfish tyrant who wishes everything for herself and grudges any advantage to anyone else. As we know, Goethe shared this opinion. He valued much in the English, particularly in individual Englishmen, but from a political point of view he considered them a cold-hearted nation of shopkeepers, as could be proved by fifty quotations. I will only refer to the one on the slave trade in the essay on England. Goethe expected a lasting peace only from a strong Germany:

> "And if all thought as I think, soon would the power be there
> Opposing the power, and all would be blessèd by peace."

These words might have been written for the present war. Germany's firm desire for peace, which has been maintained for forty-four years up to the limits of the bearable—even beyond these limits—was insufficient to keep it. This peace can only be enforced by the preponderance of Germany, the only country in Europe that seriously desires peace. And Goethe knew exactly how this power is to be obtained:

> "In unity be strong,
> And none can equal you."

And the words which he wrote for 1815 will—by the grace of God—have a still higher significance for the year 1915:

> "And everywhere, on every side
> We burst the foreign yoke;
> And now we're Germans far and wide,
> A free and mighty folk.
> And thus we were and still remain
> The noblest of all races,
> Of honest heart and pure of stain,
> Do justice in all places."

The "honest heart" is the truthfulness which is at present so striking in the midst of the inferno of lies heaped upon lies. "Do justice in all places" is the strict honesty of the whole German policy. In all this, Goethe does not show a trace of sentimentality. In August, 1815, he replied to a rather discouraging description: "Whatever evil may befall the French, they are heartily welcome to it." That is a different Goethe to the weakly caricature which is generally drawn abroad and, unfortunately, frequently in Germany. Above all things Germans should get to know themselves, and that is the first step towards love; and, therefore, a much more intensive study of Goethe should be recommended them. And I could quote examples of terrifying ignorance in otherwise well-educated persons; such a state of affairs is nothing less than a crime against the life of the nation, a sign of contempt for the highest gifts of God. What nation ever possessed such a man? A poet of such inexhaustible power, so deep a thinker, such an excellent, firm, efficient, devoted worker.

"And what can cause more grief to noble mind
Than to see duty and, by force, be blind?"

Wisdom flows from his mouth as from an inexhaustible spring, accessible to all, beneficial to all, helpful to all, improving all, ennobling all. In this man one comes into contact with New Germany, which is so little known, which has been born again, in its most noble incorporation. Humane and, at the same time, of relentless severity, his heart open to the whole universe and yet firmly rooted in the "fatherland of the noblest race," worshipping democratic equality from early youth up to the highest age, and yet the self-sacrificing servant of a prince, free from all dogmatic restrictions and deeply religious in reverence and trustful faith; a poet, painter, friend of music, no less a zealous student of natural science, technical arts and industries, of commercial problems, earlier than any other man—Goethe, who died in 1832, predicted the teansformation of the world by railways and telegraph, for his spirit pressed forward in the youthful joy of Germany's awakening from her slumber. Thus in the first hour of the dawn of the new mighty Empire this new ideal of humanity was set up before us; the perfect German man. For I repeat: the Old Germany of Walter von der Vogelweide still exists, but has become a New Germany, otherwise it would not live, or would live only as an aged, toothless, tottering man; but from its trance it has arisen as the youngest and most vigorous of all states in the world. Goethe knew this as he knew all things:

"And prince and people, all and all,
Are fresh once more and new!
As liberty will come to you,
The freedom of your call."

Because, therefore, in spite of the half-mediæval external decoration, which deceived the ignorant, everything in Germany is so astonishingly "fresh and new," and because concentration is required to feel free and at ease in the "national meaning," and not in the foreign accepted sense, I should recommend every German who feels himself hurt by foreign hate, to pay no heed to the envy and hate of others, but, in the first place, to be content to know himself better and love himself in a proper manner. Germany has need of a great deal of internal strength, in order to construct a political and social organisation equal to the already existing military organisation, and for some time to come she will have to dispense with "love." For all the social and political measures which will have to be introduced will not be in accordance with the taste of the leader-writers on the Thames, Seine, Neva, and Tiber. Much will be misunderstood; Germany will be much abused and many lies published about her. This cannot be changed. Benefits, recognition, assistance, flattery, self-denial thrown away either on states or individuals never assure love. We have seen it in regard to certain men who owed Germany everything. And how much greater progress Germany would have made in Alsace-Lorraine if she had followed Cromwell's precept in Ulster and not the dictates of a weakly humanitarianism. And all the explaining and excusing which is now so much in vogue I consider useless; it only breeds worse impertinence, *qui s'excuse s'accuse* still remains true. Do what is right and let the world talk. How fine it would have been if the Germans after a short notification to Belgium had simply marched into the country; no inquiries in England, no official excuses, the initiated knew, then, what the whole world knows now. It would soon have been cleared up and the effect, whilst preserving all our dignity, would have been much more powerful. It was but a new phase of the conflict of what Carlyle so aptly calls " noble German veracity and obstinate Flemish cunning." I wish the Germans could make up their minds for ten years not to read a line of what is written about them abroad. It would save them an enormous amount of time and annoyance. And in the meanwhile work at themselves, get to know themselves more thoroughly, boldly cast out the many foreign things which take up so much room in Germany, become pure German. The German army is a pure German invention and creation, inspired with a pure German spirit. All ignoble or false elements are either carried away or cast out. Would that the same might succeed in political as well as in social, intellectual, and artistic life. Would that, for instance, Berlin, the temple of the General Staff, might cease to be the resort of the worst class of swindlers, and the seat of the most disgusting decay of morals. Let us not forget Carlyle's saying about "the disgust at the worthlessness of men." For that we need no ostracism, no watch committee;

such measures are not German. But we do need deep and serious reflection on ourselves, severe self-education of the mind and taste, as the army supplies it for the character, followed—as it cannot be otherwise—by a relentless rejection of all that is foreign and repugnant to the pure, high, German mind. Suddenly, it will be found that more and more among the noble and wise of all countries will follow the example of Montaigne and Carlyle; that they will no longer judge Germany externally and superficially, but, in humility and confidence, study her language and her character, and so learn to love her. Love never comes from the quarter and at the time it is expected; the Divine sower goes His own ways, and it is His will that we should receive the best from Him. We, who live to-day, will not experience this great transformation from hate to love; but the day will come, I, a foreigner, announce it from the depths of a well-founded and unshakeable conviction.

Ingram Content Group UK Ltd.
Milton Keynes UK
UKHW021943290623
424309UK00005B/75